S0-AGC-205

SCHOOL OF EDUCATION
CURRICULUM LABORATORY
UM-DEARBORN

THE AMERICAN PEOPLE

O   *The Native American People of the East*

O   *The Native American People of the West*

O   *The American People in Colonial New England*

O   *The American People in the Colonial South*

O   *The American People in the Antebellum North*

O   *The American People in the Antebellum South*

●   *The American People on the Western Frontier*

O   *The American People in the Industrial City*

O   *The American People in the Depression*

O   *The American People in the Age of Kennedy*

SCHOOL OF EDUCATION
CURRICULUM LABORATORY
UM-DEARBORN

The American People On the Western Frontier

Edited by
P. RICHARD METCALF

James Axtell, Series Editor

SCHOOL OF EDUCATION
CURRICULUM LABORATORY
UM-DEARBORN

P

Pendulum Press, Inc.

West Haven, Connecticut

COPYRIGHT © 1973 BY PENDULUM PRESS, INC.
All Rights Reserved

Clothbound Edition ISBN 0-88301-082-8 Complete Set
0-88301-089-5 This Volume

Paperback Edition ISBN 0-88301-066-6 Complete Set
0-88301-073-9 This Volume

Library of Congress Catalog Card Number 72-95871

Published by
Pendulum Press, Inc.
The Academic Building
Saw Mill Road
West Haven, Connecticut 06516

Printed in the United States of America

Cover Design by Dick Brassil, Silverman Design Group
Cover Print Courtesy The Bettmann Archive

CONTENTS

ABOUT THE EDITOR

P. Richard Metcalf graduated *magna cum laude* from Northwestern University, received an M.A. degree from Yale University and is currently completing the requirements for a Ph.D. at Yale. He is also on the faculty there as an instructor in history and American Studies, teaching a seminar on Indian history and customs. Mr. Metcalf has contributed numerous articles to a forthcoming volume, *Encyclopedia of the West.*

ABOUT THE SERIES EDITOR

James Axtell, the recipient of a B.A. degree from Yale University and a Ph.D. from Cambridge University, has also studied at Oxford University and was a postdoctoral fellow at Harvard University. Mr. Axtell has taught history at Yale and is currently Associate Professor of Anglo-American History at Sarah Lawrence College. He is on the editorial board of *History of Education Quarterly* and has been a consultant to the American Council of Learned Societies. He has published several articles and reviews and is the author of a forthcoming book, *The School upon a Hill: Education and Society in Colonial New England.*

ACKNOWLEDGMENTS

Grateful acknowledgment is made to the authors and publishers who granted permission to reprint the following selections:

The Autobiography of Theodore Edgar Potter, by T. E. Potter. Published by G.C. Sprague.

A Bride Goes West, by N.T. Anderson and H.H. Smith. Reprinted by permission of International Famous Agency.

The Buckeye Rovers in the Gold Rush, edited by Howard L. Scamehorn. Reprinted by permission of Ohio University Press.

Gambler's Wife: The Life of Malinda Jenkins, edited by Jesse Lilienthal. Reprinted by permission of the editor.

The Life of an Ordinary Woman, by Anne Ellis. Reprinted by permission of Houghton Mifflin Company.

Religion on the American Frontier, volume II, by William Warren Sweet. Copyright ©1936, by Harper & Row, Publishers, Inc. By permission of the publishers.

A Texas Cowboy or *Fifteen Years on the Hurricane Deck of a Spanish Pony,* by Charles A. Siringo. Reprinted by permission of University of Nebraska Press.

We Sagebrush Folks, by Annie P. Greenwood. Published by Hawthorne Books.

FOREWORD

The American People is founded on the belief that the study of history in the schools and junior levels of college generally begins at the wrong end. It usually begins with abstract and pre-digested *conclusions*—the conclusions of other historians as filtered through the pen of a textbook writer—and not with the primary sources of the past and unanswered *questions*—the starting place of the historian himself.

Since we all need, use, and think about the past in our daily lives, we are all historians. The question is whether we can be skillful, accurate, and useful historians. The only way to become such is to exercise our historical skills and interests until we gain competence. But we have to exercise them in the same ways the best historians do or we will be kidding ourselves that we are *doing* history when in fact we are only absorbing sponge-like the results of someone else's historical competence.

Historical competence must begin with one crucial skill—the ability to distinguish between past and present. Without a sharp sense of the past as a different time from our own, we will be unable to accord the people of the past the respect that we would like to receive from the people of the future. And without according them that respect, we will be unable to recognize their integrity as individuals or to understand them as human beings.

A good sense of the past depends primarily on a good sense of the present, on experience, and on the imaginative empathy to relate ourselves to human situations not our own. Although most students have had a relatively brief experience of life and have not yet given full expression to their imaginative sympathies, they do possess the one essential prerequisite for the study of history—the lives they have lived from birth to young adulthood. This should be the initial focus of their study of the past, not remotely adult experiences to which they cannot yet relate, such as politics, diplomacy, and war.

Thus the organizing perspective of this series is the universal life experiences that all people have: being born, growing up, loving and marrying, working and playing, behaving and misbehaving, worshipping, and dying. As only he could, Shakespeare portrayed these cycles in *As You Like It* (Act II, scene vii):

> All the world's a stage,
> And all the men and women merely players.
> They have their exits and their entrances;
> And one man in his time plays many parts,
> His acts being seven ages. At first the infant,
> Mewling and puking in the nurse's arms.
> And then the whining school-boy, with his satchel
> And shining morning face, creeping like snail
> Unwillingly to school. And then the lover,
> Sighing like furnace, with a woeful ballad
> Made to his mistress' eyebrow. Then a soldier,
> Full of strange oaths, and bearded like a pard;
> Jealous in honour, sudden and quick in quarrel,
> Seeking the bubble reputation
> Even in the cannon's mouth. And then the justice,
> In fair round belly with good capon lined,
> With eyes severe and beard of formal cut,
> Full of wise saws and modern instances;
> And so he plays his part. The sixth age shifts
> Into the lean and slipper'd pantaloon,
> With spectacles on nose and pouch on side;
> His youthful hose, well saved, a world too wide
> For his shrunk shank; and his big manly voice,
> Turning again toward childish treble, pipes
> And whistles in his sound. Last scene of all,
> That ends this strange eventful history,
> Is second childishness, and mere oblivion,
> Sans teeth, sans eyes, sans taste, sans everything.

These are experiences to which any student can relate and from which he can learn, simply because they surround him daily in his home, community, and not least, school.

There is an additional reason for focussing on the universal life cycle. If history is everything that happened in the past, obviously some things were and are more important than others. Until fairly recently the things historians have found important have been the turning points or *changes* in history—"great" men and "great" events. But recently, with the help of anthropologists, historians have come to a greater awareness of the importance of stability and inertia, of *non-change* in society. For every society—and therefore its history—is a mixture of change and stability, of generally long periods of fixity punctuated now and then by moments of modification and change.

The major reason for the stability of society is the conservative bent of human behavior and ideals, the desire to preserve, hold, fix, and keep stable. People acquire habits and habits impede change. The habits people acquire are the common ways the members of a society react to the world—how they behave and feel and think in common—which distinguish them from other societies and cultures. So at bottom history is about ordinary people, how they did things alike and together that gave continuity and durability to their society so that it could change to meet new circumstances without completely losing its former identity and character.

America is such a society and *The American People* is an attempt to provide representative selections from primary sources about the lives and habits of ordinary people in periods of history that are usually known in textbooks for their great changes.

Since the experience of each student is the only prerequisite for the study of primary sources at the first level, annotations and introductory material have been reduced to a minimum, simply enough to identify the sources, their authors, and the circumstances in which they were written.

But the remains of the past are mute by themselves. Many sources have survived that can tell us what happened in the past and why, but they have to be questioned properly to reveal their secrets. So by way of illustration, a number of questions have been asked in each chapter, but these should be supplemented by the students whose experiences and knowledge and interests are, after all, the flywheel of the educational process. Although the questions and sources are divided into chapters, they should be used freely in the other chapters; the collection should be treated as a whole. And although most of the illustrative questions are confined to the sources at hand, questions that extend to the present should be asked to anchor the acquired knowledge of the past in the immediate experience of the present. Only then will learning be real and lasting and history brought to life.

INTRODUCTION

From the founding of Jamestown to the beginning of the twentieth century, the unsettled frontier played a major role in the history of the American people. The acquisition, exploration, and settlement of western lands have even been called the unique aspect of our national experience. The frontier was an ever-moving, ever-changing phenomenon. During colonial times the Appalachian Mountains were the western frontier. By 1800, the frontier was the Ohio valley, and by 1830, settlement had reached the Mississippi. In the next twenty-five years the frontier jumped to California and the West Coast, and then rolled back on itself so that by 1890, there was no place left that could be called frontier.

Each frontier area was opened by different types of people seeking different things. The great majority of the pioneers in all parts of the country were farmers, regardless of their nationality or background, and were most interested in finding just enough good land to support themselves and their families. But other goals drew other people. The Rocky Mountains were opened up by hunters after beaver fur. California was inundated by swarms of gold-seekers from the cities of the eastern seaboard. The Salt Lake deserts were settled by members of a church searching for freedom from religious persecution. The list is endless and the point clear—the settlement of the frontier was a long and complex process.

Today, the frontier era is remembered as a period of high adventure, romance, and great stirring deeds. A large portion of our popular literature and entertainment media is given over to stories and re-creations of incidents in frontier history. Many Americans are more familiar with Custer's Last Stand, the Great Cattle Drives, the

Defense of the Alamo, the California Gold Rush, or the Gunfight at the OK Corral than they are with the details of the American Revolution or even the last presidential election. And probably more people know the names of Davy Crockett and Daniel Boone than know the names of their own senators in Congress.

The dramatic episodes and great heroes, however, were but a small part of the history of the frontier. Most pioneers felt their lives to be neither adventurous nor romantic and would have been surprised to learn that a later age would call them heroes. They are a hard people to come to know, for the struggles of frontier life prevented most of them from recording day-to-day events, and there were few newsmen in frontier communities. A number of pioneers on all frontiers did keep diaries or journals, however, and still others in later years set down their reminiscences when they discovered that the world was interested in what they had done. The source material in this book is excerpted from a number of these journals and reminiscences, and provides two opportunities for the student of history: (1) he can compare the different kinds of sources and evaluate their validity as accurate accounts of past events; (2) in reading of what the pioneers themselves thought important in their lives, he may, perhaps, sense the reality of a part of our history which has come to be shrouded in myth.

I. BIRTH

Childbearing on the frontiers could easily be a time of joy or tragedy. It was very seldom that a mother could call on the help of a qualified physician. Who was called in place of a doctor? What kind of care did the mother and new baby receive? What was the father's role at birth? How much did pioneer women seem to know about having babies before the time came? What were the women's attitudes toward giving birth? Were there any rituals or social customs attached to birth? How were babies fed? What were the dangers of childbirth and infancy? Were girl babies regarded differently from boys?

Malinda Jenkins

Malinda Jenkins was born on an Indiana farm in 1848 and spent the first years of her married life on the Missouri and Kansas frontiers. The following passages are excerpted from her autobiography. (Jesse Lilienthal, ed., Gambler's Wife: The Life of Malinda Jenkins *(1933, 47-49, 53, 112-14.)*

And as time went on the changes come. I'd been married the first day of April and next year, come the twenty-fifth of May, we had our baby. It made quite a difference with the old lady; she begin to mellow on me.

Willie had been staying pretty close at home and looking for this. On Monday morning he asked me, 'How do you feel?' and I said, 'Fine.' I did, I told the truth.

15

The corn was planted and Willie hadn't nothing to do. 'How about my goin' fishin', Linney, for two or three hours down the Eel?'

It was only a little ways off and I was glad to have him go. But he wasn't gone an hour until I was about as sick a woman as anyone'd ever want to see—and all alone.

We had a pen of unshucked corn, say a couple of hundred foot off from the house, that Willie had sold to Mahoney, our nearest neighbor. Mahoney wanted to get a load of it; he sent his wife, old Katy, up to shuck it, to have it ready when he drove over.

She was outside there working but I hadn't seen her. I was feeling so bad I commenced striding up and down. I didn't know what to do. I went to crying out loud and she heard me. In she come and I was certainly glad to see her.

She asked me, 'Do you know what's the matter with you, Mrs. Page?'

'I think I do, I reckon I'm goin' to have my baby.'

That dear old lady trotted nearly all the three miles to my doctor-sister Betty's. They come back riding double.

Betty put me to bed and about two in the afternoon Willie come and him and Betty stuck their heads together. Betty thought I'd better have a man doctor so Willie went over to New Maysville, across Eel River, for old Doc Long that attended to papa and the family as far back as I could remember.

A woman that was expecting had to take good care that she had plenty fixed to eat for her neighbors when they got there. There was no telling how long they was in for. There wasn't no paying these friends so you had to treat them good.

Them days there wasn't no twilight sleep. We had children natural and stood our misery. Doc Long told Betty, 'I think everything is goin' to be all right but I don't like her bein' so long.' That was Wednesday night.

He give me something that eased me entirely. Maybe, it was chloroform. I went to sleep and after a while when the pains commenced again I hollered for more of that stuff. I was talking silly and off my head. Finally he give me another whiff but that was all.

About three o'clock, Thursday morning, Ollie was born; he weighed more than nine pounds. . . . When my papa heard as I'd had a young 'un, he cried. I was only eighteen, he didn't like that part of it. 'A child has a child,' was what he said.

Mama Page showed up when the baby come and took care of me like one of her own. Being a granny makes a lot of difference. . . .

I was young and healthy and everything went fine. Only for one thing: I give too much milk. Ollie couldn't take it all and my breasts got sore. Lumps come in them. The old lady was scared and sent for the doctor. He wouldn't use turpentine—it takes the soreness out but it dries up the milk. He tried camphor but it didn't help none.

One day he asked mama Page did she know any place where she could get hold of a puppy. I heard him. 'What!' I said, 'do you want me to raise a dog with my boy?'

'It's the best way, with no one to come here and draw off your milk.' And by crikey! If he didn't start out to find one, and come back with a female fox terrier—a little thing, a right young puppy! I put it to the breast and it sucked just as easy as the baby.

Ollie, when he begin to get a little old, would reach over and get hold of the pup's ear and pull it; I had to take Ollie and hold his hands. When the baby went to growing and the dog, too, it's the truth, I had an armful!

(HER SECOND CHILD CAME TWO YEARS LATER.)

Baby May was born the first day of November, on a blue sky Monday morning. Old Aunt Mary McCloud come to help out. I didn't have a hard time at all, and when they put her in my arms and I looked down into that little baby's face, I told her, 'You won't have to work like mama if she can help it.' And I said to Willie, 'The boy's your'n but the girl's mine!' A feeling come over me that May was going to be with me always, much closer than anybody else. That turned out to be true.

Aunt Mary didn't know how to take care of the baby, loving and playing with her, but not keeping her clean. I told Willie I didn't want her around. 'If you can't go after your mother account of the bad roads, you watch Ollie and fix your meals, and I'll tend to May.'

I washed her good with castile soap, and I put a little starch on her skin—that's all I had—to soothe her sore spots. I took some soot off the fireplace and dusted her with it. Inside twenty-four hours she was healing up. It's as good as anything I know to cure inflammation. But it's mighty hard to get now. Soot ain't so common as it was.

When May was six weeks old we took her down for Willie's people to see her—thirty miles distant. Called on them all. Mama Page fell for her. She liked her black hair and blue eyes—I got on to that right away. They was all crazy over her, swore that she looked just like the Pages—and she did, she was the spit image of them. They all had the same hair and eyes. And I didn't mind, I wanted May to look like Willie; he was a handsome man.

(AFTER ELEVEN MORE YEARS THE FAMILY WAS LIVING IN A KANSAS COW TOWN, MALINDA HAD BEEN DIVORCED AND REMARRIED.)

How happy we was and business so good—until the curse of sickness come along. Typhoid broke out from not having proper sanitary conditions. There was only one doctor; he was a good one too, but just up against it, poor fellow. He didn't know what to do for nurses or nothing.

Yes, I felt sorry for him—he come over to my tent and told me: 'I understand you're a good nurse, Mrs. Chase, and a benevolent woman. Will you undertake to care for a family that's in terrible straits? You go up the street till you come to this number'—the tents all had numbers—'and you'll find a pitiful state of things. The woman's layin' in bed and don't know nothin'. Her baby is by her side. A widow woman, and only a seven-year old daughter to take care of her and the baby. I ain't easy affected but I sure took it home to myself—it's enough to break your heart to see it.'

I said, 'I'll see to it right off.' I went to three or four women that I was acquainted with. Two was willing to go with me and that was enough for once.

I never, never will forget how I felt when I got there. The little girl was standing at the flap of the tent; she was very polite, a smart little girl. 'Good mornin',' I said, 'are you alone?'

'No, mama is in bed.' I asked how her mama was.

'I don't know, she ain't spoke to me.'

'Where's the baby?'

'Abed with mama.'

I walked in and turned the cover down from off the child. The light hurt his eyes and it made him blink. But pretty soon he began to coo and laugh and maybe them little baby smiles didn't go to my heart! And them big blue eyes!

He was wrapped up in what they used to call a breakfast shawl, just little colored affairs that women wore around their shoulders, very common of that day. I picked him up. I asked the women with me, would they be willing to tend the mother. 'If you'll look after the sick woman, I'll take the baby home and send a basket of groceries over from my husband's store.' I said, 'Don't give her one thing in the world to eat. No matter how much she begs, give her nothing but water.' I knew enough about typhoid and how feeding could kill people.

Well now, about this child. I fed him on condensed milk and he done good. May was a sleepy head, a young girl then not twelve, but believe me she'd get up at night to warm milk for the baby and glad to do it. It wasn't hard to love little Frankie.

When his mother was almost well she told me she wanted me to keep him. She'd had a terrible time. They come out to Wichita Falls when her brother wrote for them, but by the time they got there he'd sold out his cattle ranch and moved off and she hadn't no idea where he was. Then her husband died two months after little Frankie was born. She was plain stranded: took in washing for a living for her and the two children.

I kept that child a year and three months.

One day his mother come to me. 'Mrs. Chase,' she said, 'I know it will hurt you awful but I'm goin' to leave it to you to answer. You was one of the causes of savin' my life, and I ain't forgettin' what you done for Frankie.' She was afeared to come out with it. 'Some people I was washin' for here, went to Kansas City and run into my brother. Here's his letter that jes' come.'

He wrote her, 'Following this letter will be some money on the way, and you and your children can come to us. Bring the baby even if you have to ask the people to give him back to you.' Him and his wife had no youngsters of their own and it was plain to me they wanted the woman most for her children. 'It's up to you,' she said;

'you ain't adopted him but I said you might.' Of course, I let her take the child.

Frankie thought I was his mother. He was crazy about May, too—and she over him. He was beginning to crawl around and walk now. And here was the cutest thing about him. He'd set in the middle of my lap at table, hungry as a wild cat, and wanting to get started. Set there panting, with his mouth open and his small hands fanning the air, but I'd learned him not to put them on the plate. God, the first dinner we set down to after he was gone, I thought it was all over with me. I couldn't swallow a mouthful; I looked over and seen my May. She hadn't et and the tears was rolling down her cheeks. I jumped up and left the table. . . .

Mr. Chase said, 'I know how you feel; I feel that way myself.'

I got two letters. The brother wrote me the most beautiful letter, thanking me and saying how I would be repaid a thousand times. And I have been. The other was from the mother. I never heard from them but that once; I don't know what become of little Frankie.

Annie Greenwood

Annie Greenwood was the daughter of a well-to-do doctor in Salt Lake City. In the 1880s, she married and went to live on a pioneer farm in the Snake River plain of Idaho, where she became a school-teacher for her neighbors. (Annie P. Greenwood, We Sagebrush Folks *(1934), 131-36.)*

I was determined to go to the hospital at Twin Falls to be confined. I had seen enough of that surly sheep-doctor, and there was no other physician in that part of the country. Besides, there was something seriously wrong with me. I suffered eclampsia after the birth of Walter, almost losing my life, and my arms were acting in the same way as they had before he came. They were even worse, for they were not only without sense of touch, but they were filled with unbearable pain.

One evening I was walking the floor in terrible agony, cradling one arm on the other in an effort to ease them. I wore, having removed my daytime clothes, a long, flowing blue-green kimona, covered with golden butterflies. I had made it myself, before coming to Idaho, and it had a way of bringing the best out of my blue-green eyes and my fluffy light-brown hair. But as I paced the floor, I had no thought of how I looked. A woman in the last months of pregnancy does not expect to present a beautiful sight.

The children were asleep. Early September had brought a cool night, and it was already dark. Through the kitchen door I heard Charley's footsteps with a different, quicker spring to them. His eyes were bright as he came into the room.

"You don't mind if I go over to the Mormon dance at Lateral Eight with the Currys, do you? I knew you wouldn't want to go."

What could I say to that eager voice? I am afraid I lied, though I did not mean it for a lie. I said I did not mind, and I did. I minded being left all alone in that quiet farm-house when I was in such pain. I minded being the one left behind because I was the one to bear a child, and I loved to dance. I walked the floor, still cradling my aching arms, crying to myself, for no one could hear me but myself, and no one ever knew it until this moment.

Yes, Charley had failed me. He had no business to leave me there alone under such circumstances. But he would never have done it had I not failed him in some way first. We women build the foundation for men's treatment of us. Some of our men need more love than we give them, and some of them need a right good beheading every once in a while. Many a woman wrongs her husband with too little affection. And many a woman wrongs her man with too much patience. But if there need be one wrong or the other, let it be that of too much patience. For sometimes the long road of all-kindness conquers at last.

I had uremic poisoning. I had suffered from it ever since my eleventh year, when I contracted a severe case of measles which crippled my kidneys so that the uric-acid crystals were returned to the blood-stream. I was drowsy nearly all the time. I grew tired so soon. I never knew vigorous health. But this state had been mine so long that I imagined everyone felt the same way; so I neither questioned it nor complained, and thus was my danger the greater. I lived constantly with death at my elbow.

It was likely to get me this time. But I went on, trying to be a normal creature, a farm woman, a super-human, believing that all I did was no more than I should do. The week before Rhoda was born I cooked for fifteen men who had come to help stack hay. And in the intervals of serving them I would creep into my bedroom to sink for a moment across my bed. I was so tired. Through the bedroom window I could see the mare and the cow, turned out to pasture for weeks because they were going to have young.

The day came when I was packing my trunk to leave for Twin Falls. I had been cleaning the house, so as to leave it decent for the little family, and I had washed. The last piece of my ironing lay across the ironing-board, and my trunk stood open to receive it. The little baby things were lying in one of the top compartments. I thought I would feed my thirty-two chicks for the last time. They were to be fall fries.

I had the wire chicken-house near the canal. Nine o'clock, and still light, with the long twilight of a hill-top that looks afar at mountains across a vast sweep of valley. I had set Charley's supper for him, as he had been late in the fields, and he had just started eating it.

I was crouched among the restless little fluff-balls, sprinkling wheat from a can, when the bag that acts as a cushion for the head of the child broke, the water flowing downhill. This should not have occurred for another week, nor until after labor. I had been working too hard. With a feeling of dazed incredulity, I stood up and turned back to the house. No chance of getting to the hospital. More than dismay, disappointment, made my heart heavy for the moment. But I walked into the living-room, where Charley sat eating and looking over an old paper, and said, "The baby is coming. You'd better go for the doctor."

He looked at my face, and knew. In a few moments I heard the Mormon white-top rattle past the front of the house, where we then had a driveway. By this time labor had set in, and it was not coming gradually, but with violence whose power made me realize that my time was not far off. I went into the bedroom, carrying my baby's little clothes, made of cloth purchased from the same baby bazaar that had provided the material for the other children's baby clothes. The school money had come in handy there, and I had sewed them myself. I had to buy little shirts and bands to take the place of those given to the Curry baby.

Clean sheets I put on the bed, and water on the range, first filling the fire-box with sagebrush and lighting it. I set about these things restlessly because the pains were absorbing my attention. I gave no thought to the possibility of my baby being born with no help at hand. I waste very little time on possible difficulties.

But I was not alone, after all. The rushing sound of wheels grating on the gravel of the driveway came to a stop at the porch with the toothpick pillars. Feet on the porch boards, the door-screen closing after three figures, blurred in the deepening darkness for I had carried the glass lamp to the bedroom. The sheep-doctor and "another woman" to care for me.

The doctor had left his ewes, which were doing some out-of-season lambing, and he was not very happy about leaving them. His attitude expressed the outrage of one who considered that I might have planned better. I was perfectly heartless. The only thing that concerned me was the bringing of that child into the world, and I was the helpless agent of powerful Nature, robbed of the right to will.

Rhoda was born. "A girl," announced the sheep-doctor, in a grudging voice. I was too tired to care what sort of voice he used. I had not expected him to break down and cry with joy. A little girl! I was glad, but so tired. She had come, and now I could rest.

As part of his treatment the doctor used a catheter. From that moment there was a terrible pain in the back of my head. It never ceased, day or night. It was unbearable torture. Unbearable, therefore I need not bear it. It is only the little things that can hurt us. It is only the little things we have to bear. When an injury is great enough, Nature supplies her own anaesthesia. I lapsed into unconsciousness after a week of suffering.

The fourteenth day of my lying there thus, my young husband demanded of the sheep-doctor, "What shall I do with her? She is getting no better. Shall I take her to the hospital at Twin Falls?"

"Foolish expense," muttered the sheep-doctor, who was really not a bad-natured man, but an eccentric. "Foolish expense. If she's going to get well, she'll get well right here. If she's going to die, you'll have all that useless expense."

For years I held that against the sheep-doctor. I thought he was heartless. But as it turned out, he was right. The doctor into whose hands I fell at the hospital was far less competent than my sheep-doctor, even though he was of the school of medicine practised by my father, the allopath, and the sheep-doctor the despised homeopath. For when the hospital doctor had not guessed right after several tries, he said I was just having an attack of hysteria. He thought he could bring me out of it the way he had cured another woman patient. When she had failed to respond to his treatment, he had turned down the covers and spanked her, and she had been so mad she cried, and was well at once.

That was a far crueler implication than any made by the sheep-doctor. After all, the hospital doctor did not cure me. He had no hand in my cure whatever. He did not even know what was the matter with me.

Anne Ellis

Anne Ellis was the wife of a hard rock miner, and lived in the frontier mining towns of the central Colorado Rockies in the 1890s. (Anne Ellis, The Life of an Ordinary Woman *(1929), 179-87.)*

And I? I am a bride, and when I look back over my life, though I hate self-pity, my heart aches for this poor girl. Nothing to do with. Joe sends us a pair of wool blankets and a set of knives and forks. My furniture is all home-made, table, bed, and shelves. The tiny stove is set up on blocks of wood; there is a shelf for the water bucket; my plates against the wall; the knives and forks where they will show; the Chinese platter brightening up one corner; the pansy picture doing its part; white sugar sacks hemstitched for a table cover; and we are started. I have always wanted things, but never so much as then. It was a hard, dreary time. From the first I am pregnant; married on the fourth of October, my baby is born on the Fourth of July. Ed Howe says, when he comes to this place in a woman's story, he lays the book down. I suppose he doesn't like it; neither did I.

One morning George is peeved (only we didn't have this word then—we would have said, 'on the prod') at out little stove, which refuses to draw, and he kicks the door off; the fire burns just as bright, still, there is a coolness for a few days. I find it is hard to keep him in a good humor. The time goes, cooking, cleaning, washing, and ironing; no amusements except planning what we will do when the mine is sold. They take out ore all the time and it is good, but not enough to pay.

All this first winter, George is trying to train me. I find men who have led a wild life are more exacting of their own womenkind. I expect they have seen so many tough women they have lost faith. One day we have a time over my saying 'darn.' He didn't intend to have his woman swearing. To-day I have an enlarged throat. It may have come from swallowing, or trying to, the lump which would rise in it. It would have been better had I quarreled, but, when a small child, listening to Mama and Henry and seeing how foolish and useless it all was, I decided there would be no quarreling in my home. In my small mind I saw it was she who started them and none of them helped, only making it miserable for us children. And, quarreling fathers and mothers, these children listening to you are more hurt and miserable and ashamed than you realize.

Afterward, when we moved to Cripple Creek, things are running smoother. I say, 'We seem to be getting along better'; his answer was, 'Yes, you are getting some sense.' But I wasn't; I was only learning to manage him without his knowing it; also the use of 'hot air' and 'soft soap.'

Then Christmas is coming. I so want to send the children something, and go to Gunnison, walking up and down the stores longing to buy so many things. As I call to mind now, I had something like two dollars to spend. I think I got the boys knives, and a little white workbox for Jose, which I took home to paint a rose on the lid, and this was the extent of my purchases.

In the spring I am given thirty-five dollars and go to Gunnison to buy furniture. With it I get a bed and mattress, a rocking-chair and two other chairs, a mirror, lace curtains, and have three dollars left. With this, I intend to feed my soul, and spend it all in house plants; they do make a brave showing in the windows with the new curtains. I color some gunny-sacks red (it always rubs off) for a rug, sew little pieces of silk in circles and make a lambrequin for the shelves on which my books and pictures are placed, and drape an old box for a dresser, hanging the new mirror over it and am quite 'decked out.'

Then there is the child coming, a mingled pleasure and sorrow. Now I will have something really my own, something to love and cling to, but how to get clothes ready, what to make them of, how to care for it? This first wardrobe was made of the white outing-flannel wedding dress, a pink cotton dress of mine, and flour sacks. All the rags one could save, a piece of real linen from a man's white shirt, a bar of castile soap, a bottle of vaseline, and some safety pins were the outfit. These and a twisted twine string were packed in a box all ready. Rosie had helped me.

Now comes the third of July; there is to be a picnic in Iris, and I am determined to go. George never cares to go anywhere, but I coax for his permission to let me go, which was given, so I make two big blueberry cakes for my share of the lunch. We would go in freight wagons, but this is good enough, and I can probably sit with the driver on the spring seat. When I get up the morning of the Fourth, I feel strange, and soon start to have pains. They grow worse and worse; still I pack my lunch and dress, not intending to let a little stomach-ache stand in the way of my going to that picnic. But I am no better, so go and tell Rosie, 'Guess I won't go.' She knows at once, and says, 'Well—I guess you have knocked that picnic in the head for both of us. Go home and I will come over later.'

She comes, fixes the bed and lays out the contents of the little box, and sees that there is hot water. All this day I suffer, both Rosie and George helping me as much as they can, and at four in the evening Neita is born, the first child in Chance. 'Deacon' Hurley had gone by the house at noon, heard me screaming, and would not return that way; in fact, I think he went to the saloon and got drunk, but then the Deacon didn't need much of an excuse to get drunk.

George did the cooking and housework. Each day Rosie came and dressed Neita, also taking care of me—a born nurse. I have always felt I owed her a debt of gratitude.

On the third day I get very sick—such pain in my back and head. Rosie and George fill bags with hot salt and put over me, but nothing helps. At last Rosie says that we must have the doctor; she has done all she can. (Oh, we hate to have the doctor—no money to pay him!) He is sent for, and, after hours of waiting, arrives with two girls in the buggy with him. He comes in, pushing the door wide open, walks over to the bed, and, throwing back the covers, grabs the neck of my nightgown with the other hand, tears it off, scattering hot plates and bags of salt in all directions. 'Don't you see this girl is burning up with fever? It is blood poison!' At once he gets his instruments out and goes to work. It was agony. And I don't think Dr. McIntosh was ever paid either.

Foolish as I was, I knew somehow it was better for the baby to sleep alone. (All babies I had known slept with their mothers.) So she had a bed made of a soap box. Many times I would look at it, longing for a real baby bed, consoling myself with the thought that one day when we are rich and great, it will be something to tell—'My baby's first bed was a soap box.' We have become neither rich nor great, and this is the first time I have mentioned the soap box. It seems things of this sort are only a virtue when you rise above them; otherwise they are a disgrace.

Rosie insisted I stay in bed till the ninth day, which seemed foolish when I felt so well. When Neita is two weeks old, there is to be a dance, and I beg to go. We do go, taking her with us, but my pleasure is soon over. George doesn't waltz, and the first dance after we go in is a waltz. A man asks me and I can't resist and start to dance. George invites me off the floor. I sit struggling to keep the tears back through another dance, then we go home.

The inward struggle I had always had seemed to drop away now, I was so interested in Neita, and from the first she is unusually bright and good-looking.

One night before she was born a few are gathered in a cabin, among them a nice mild white-haired grandmother. Coming around the corner of the house, I see a building across the street is on fire. I run to the door and yell, 'Crail's house is burning!' Then this sweet old lady runs to the door and says, 'Damned if it ain't!' By this time I am at the house, have grabbed two full pails of water, jump down a step with them, but drop them to grasp my side, which is killing me with pain, and if I didn't have a doctor's word for it I would think Neita had been marked, because her side is covered with bright red marks like fire. I still think the doctors are right. Once I was passing a livery barn and saw two men fighting. One had just split the other's head open with a neck-yoke, and the blood was pouring in streams. I threw my hands over my face to shut out the sight and ran for home. Still, Neita's face is not marked.

Neita is growing fast, has curly golden hair, and I curl it in different places on her head, brushing it with an old toothbrush, then walk all around her to get the best effect, recurl, back off, and look again. Now, too, since we have had a payday, she has dear little gingham aprons and real shoes.

II. GROWTH

Growing up on the frontiers usually meant that a young boy or girl would have to do without many of the things that children in the settled areas took for granted. What were some of these things? Did frontier life offer anything to compensate for their loss? How would you describe a frontier childhood? What kind of education did frontier children receive? Was it adequate for their needs? What experiences did pioneers remember about their childhood after they grew up? Did frontier mobility affect the education of children? Did young people on the frontier have more and different responsibilities than children in settled areas? Did boys and girls have significantly different experiences?

Growing up on the Michigan Frontier

Theodore Potter was born on a farm in the Michigan woods in 1832. When he was in his fifties, he wrote an autobiography which was discovered among his effects and published after his death. (T. E. Potter, The Autobiography of Theodore Edgar Potter *(1913), 1-8.)*

My early life was spent like that of other boys born on the frontier. My earliest recollection is of an occurrence that happened when I was three and half years old. Our family was then living in a log house on a new farm. My parents had gone to the home of a settler two miles away, to attend a funeral, leaving me with an elder brother and sister. There was a long ladder leading from the main room to the loft above where we children slept, and in trying to climb this ladder I fell and catching one leg between the rungs broke the limb above the knee. I suffered great pain from the injury and my brother, who did not know that the leg was broken, carried me from one bed to another, my leg dangling, trying to stop my crying. It was not until four hours later that my father reached home. The nearest doctor was at Saline five miles away, and as father had to make the trip on foot through the woods in the night it was some hours before the physician arrived to find my leg badly swollen and causing me terrible pain. After the doctor had set the leg my father took a two-inch auger and, boring holes in one of the logs which formed the side of the house, drove long pegs into them and built a wide shelf and for six weeks I lay on this firm bed that could neither jar nor spring before I was allowed to get up.

Another painful recollection that comes to mind occurred not long after. The year after my accident father made the trip to Detroit with his ox team to meet some relatives of ours who were coming on from the East to locate a farm near us. The newcomers, among other possessions, brought a bright new wagon. While my father and my mother's nephew Louis Phillips, the head of the family of newcomers, were away looking at the last piece of government land left in our township I took an axe and chopped off the tongue of the new wagon. This was a serious offence and in those days the vigorous application of a green birch was the common mode of punishment for a four-year-old offender. But for the intervention of one of the newcomers, the wife of the owner of the wagon, I might not have survived the ordeal to tell this story.

Soon after this painful occurrence we moved back to Saline where my father secured work as a surveyor which took him away from home much of the time for the next two years. At that time Saline was the largest village on the old stage route between Detroit and Chicago, and when the six horse stage-coaches came in with a grand flourish, whips cracking, tin horns blowing and horses prancing, nearly every person in town was at the tavern, to see who had come or who was to go, and all business came to a standstill until the horses were changed and the stage had passed on. But even at that time the days of the stage coach were passing. I well remember when the Michigan Central Railroad was finished as far West as Ypsilanti, and in celebration of this event all were invited to attend a barbecue there. My father went and took me with him. When we reached the town, early in the day, we found the one street decorated with flags and a brass band entertaining the visitors. We visited the place where the ox was being roasted over a huge log fire, to make sure with our own eyes that we were not to be disappointed in the great dinner we had come so far to enjoy. At the depot we witnessed the arrival of the first passenger train from Detroit carrying the officers of the road together with General Cass and other prominent men who were to speak at the exercises. About two inches of light snow had fallen that morning and when the train came in view on the slight up-grade near town we saw two men sitting on opposite ends of a cross-beam in front of the engine holding large splint brooms with which they swept the light snow from the track. Such was the railroad snow-plow of sixty-five years ago. The train consisted of several flat cars loaded with passengers, and two passenger cars for the officers of the road and speakers made like the old-fashioned Concord Coaches, with doors on each side.

For a new country the crowd of people present was very large, and to a boy of eight years it was a wonderful sight. After the dinner of roast ox, baked potatoes, pumpkin pie and ginger-bread, the people formed in line behind the band and marched to the stage where the railroad officials spoke eloquently of the great growth and prospects of Michigan. As my father had just returned from a surveying trip, he was called upon for a short description of a part of the new country. On reaching home late that night, my mother asked me what I had seen and heard that day. I told her that I had seen the roasted ox, a brass band, a railroad train, two men with brooms sweeping the railroad track, and had heard General Cass and my father make speeches to the people. Such were my boyish impressions of an event that typified so much in the development of a great state.

Another event that appealed to me as of more than ordinary importance was connected with the presidential campaign of 1840. My father was a strong Whig politically, and when he learned that General Harrison, "Old Tippecanoe," was to speak at Fort Meigs in Ohio, seventy-five miles from Saline, he and a Mr. Parsons who owned a saw-mill in the village got up a party of sixty men to go that distance to hear him. The trip was made in style, the party using their own conveyance. They fitted up a huge wagon by building a platform with rows of seats upon it which they attached to a set of large wheels used to cart logs to the saw-mill. There was a flag-staff near the driver's seat from which waved the Stars and Stripes and part way up this flag-staff was a platform to which two live coons were chained. At the rear end of the wagon was a miniature log cabin in which were two barrels of cider with faucets and cups to accommodate the oft thirsty passengers. A brass band of eight pieces and a team of sixteen horses completed the jolly outfit. As the grand cavalcade passed our log house on the road I remember that my father, who was in charge as marshal, stopped it long enough for the band to play one of its favorite airs and for the men to take another drink of cider and give three cheers for "Tippecanoe and Tyler too." Then the big train moved on, to return seven days later from its campaign with no other loss than the two barrels of cider and the time that had been spent. This was my introduction to politics.

After the campaign of 1840, my father traded farms and moved three times within two years; the last time onto a well-improved farm of eighty acres near Plymouth, Wayne County, purchased of a relative who had turned Mormon, and gone to Nauvoo, Illinois. This farm had good buildings on it and was near a district school. The school was a great advantage to all of us children and we improved our opportunities during the two and a half years we remained in the locality. Previous to this we had been pretty constantly on the move (our family moved twelve times during the first ten years of my life) and when we did settle near a school, which was not often, there would soon be another moving. Two exciting events occurred during our stay at Plymouth. One was a cyclone which came in the night when we were all in bed, and carried away the roof of our house compelling us to seek shelter in the barn in the midst of a heavy rain storm. With the help of neighbors, we had a new roof on our house within two days, though we had to go to Ypsilanti for the materials. The other event, nearly a fatal one, occurred on Christmas day, 1844. A boy of about my age by the name of Clayton came to our house to get me to go with him to hunt partridges. My father and eldest brother were away, and unknown to my mother I took the old musket that my father had carried in the battle of Oswego, with its flint lock and steel ramrod, and went off hunting with Clayton. After shooting several times at squirrels and partridges, but killing none, we went to shooting at a mark. Tiring of this, we varied our sport by loading with powder only, without bullets, and firing at each other at a distance of three or four rods. In my excitement I forgot to take the steel ramrod out of the barrel after loading my gun, and when I fired the rod passed through Clayton's coat sleeve, drawing blood, but doing no serious injury. That ended the mimic warfare. We agreed to go home and keep perfectly quiet about our Christmas celebration. In 1856, I met Clayton at the State Fair in Detroit and he said he had not yet found the ramrod.

Ten days after that Christmas hunt, our family was on the move again going to the then unbroken forests of Eaton County where we were to occupy a new double log house built in advance by my father and eldest brother. To young persons who may never have seen these pioneer shanties, much less have seen one built, a description may be of interest. The only tools used were an axe, a saw and an augur, with sometimes an adz. After clearing a plot of ground sixteen by forty-eight feet, the straightest beech and elm trees, ten to twelve inches in diameter, were cut into logs sixteen and twenty feet long, and hauled to the clearing. The thickest logs were selected for the front, so that when the structure was ready for its roof the front wall would be ten feet in height and the rear wall about seven feet, giving a good pitch to the roof. Basswood trees were cut for the roof, split in half and the centers dug out like a trough. a row of these hollowed logs was laid trough-side up from the front to the rear wall, then another row was laid trough-side down overlapping the upper edges of the first tier and making a waterproof covering, without either rafters or shingles. For floors white ash trees were cut, split, lined, hewed to make straight edges, and laid. Each shanty was twenty feet long and stood eight feet from the other, both being under this one roof which gave a covered alley-way between them. The doorways were cut in the walls so as to open into this alley. The doors were made of hewn split ash, hung on wooden hinges, and closed by a wooden latch, with a piece of rawhide string to pull the latch up to open the door. Not a nail was used in the construction of these two shanties. All the money spent on them went to buy two windows, each containing six 7 x 9 panes of glass. Fireplaces were cut through the logs, and stick chimneys were built upon the outside, laid and plastered with clay.

It took four days to make the trip to the new home and required two neighbors with their ox teams to move the family, furniture, provisions and corn. Though I was not quite thirteen years old, my father sent me ahead one day in advance with a drive of stock, consisting of three cows, two yearlings, five sheep and four hogs. A neighbor's boy of about my age accompanied me and we were guided by a rough map which my father had made of the route, and by the names of the taverns where we were to spend the nights. I was allowed six days to take the stock through and was not overtaken by the teams until we reached Eaton Rapids on the fifth day. We had twelve miles to go the next day, four of them over a new road just cut through the woods which no team had ever travelled. We reached our shanty home before night, and received a warm welcome from my brother who had been left by my father to guard the place. Cheerful fires were blazing to greet the family of seven children.

As we had no fodder for the stock, and our only food was the corn in the ear which we had hauled seventy-five miles, browsing was the only hope of life for the cattle and our principal business for the next three months was in cutting down trees for them to feed on. Within two days after reaching our new home my eldest sister and myself came down with the measles, followed within the month by the rest of the children. My eldest brother had a relapse and came near dying from this disease; all his hair fell out, leaving his head as bald as a bare rock the rest of his life. In spite of our troubles we managed to clear seven acres of land and to get in spring crops, such as corn, potatoes, pumpkins, and squash. After selling his Wayne County farm and paying off the mortgage and settling other debts, my father had $300 left with which to begin life anew and make another home. But necessary expenses until a crop could be raised reduced that amount to $100 which was just enough to buy eighty acres of government land. Father decided to go to the land office at Ionia, fifty miles away, and make the purchase of our land. The evening before going he laid the one hundred silver dollars out on the cherry table, the finest piece of furniture we had, and let us handle and count over the largest amount of money we children had ever seen. After he had gone we were greatly worried for fear he would be robbed, carrying so much money alone and travelling on foot, and talked a great deal among ourselves about it until he returned on the fourth day, safe and sound, to our great relief and joy. The crops on the seven acres of new ground proved very successful and when harvested, three acres were sown at once to wheat.

During the winter my father hauled tamarack logs to the saw-mill at Eaton Rapids to be sawed into lumber for a frame barn, giving half of the lumber for the sawing, and in the spring he built the first frame barn in that part of Benton Township, Eaton County. This was in 1846. The barn was thirty by forty feet in size and in its stable my sister taught the first school in that vicinity, having seven pupils, three of whom were from our own family.

In the following July my father cut our three acres of wheat with a sickle, and I bound it and set it up. The next day he cut one acre for a neighbor, binding and setting it in shock, and taking three bushels of wheat for his pay. I went with him to do the binding. It was very hot that day and the field was surrounded by heavy timber which shut out all movement of the air. He drank frequently and freely of cold water from a nearby spring, until we finished the work. It proved to be his last day's work. He was taken very sick, became unconscious, and on the 26th day of July, 1846, we buried him in the little wheatfield on his new frontier farm at the early age of forty-eight years. He left a widow with seven small children, whose only possession was a farm of eighty acres of which only seven acres had been cleared.

As soon as my mother's two brothers, who owned fine farms near Auburn, New York, heard of my father's death, they came out to see us with the purpose of taking us all back with them to New York and caring for us. But my mother would consent to no offer of theirs. They pleaded that the family could not support themselves in such a wilderness as Michigan then was, and that they could not leave us there to starve. But she replied that all she had to live for was her seven children, the oldest now nearly seventeen and the youngest two years of age, and that as she had moved fifteen times since her marriage she did not intend to move again as long as she could keep the family together. The winter before my father's death my oldest brother and sister had been sent to Vermontville to school for one term and I was told that I should go the next winter, but my father's death put a stop to our schooling until four years later, when a district school house was built on the corner of our farm and a school opened, which greatly relieved the anxiety of my mother, lest her children should grow up without educational advantages. At the time of his death my father was planning to sell his farm and move on to the prairies of Wisconsin where he thought we could get a living easier, and this he would have done, no doubt, had he lived. But death put an end to the roving habits of eighteen years. My mother firmly decided to stay where she was as long as her children would stay with her.

Texas Boyhood

Charles Siringo grew up on the Peninsula of Matagordo, at the extreme southern tip of Texas. (Charles A. Siringo, A Texas Cowboy; Or, Fifteen Years on the Hurricane Deck of a Spanish Pony *(1885), 7-17.)*

My father who died when I was only a year old, came from the sunny clime of Italy, while my dear old mother drifted from the Boggs of good "ould" Ireland. Am I not a queer conglomerate—a sweet-scented mixture indeed!

Our nearest neighbor was a kind old soul by the name of John Williams, whose family consisted of his wife and eleven children.

In the fall of 1859 I took my first lessons in school, my teacher being a Mr. Hale from Illinois.

The school house, a little old frame building, stood off by itself, about a mile from the Settlement, and we little tow-heads, sister and I, had to hoof it up there every morning, through the grassburrs, barefooted; our little sunbrowned feet had never been incased in shoe-leather up to that time.

To avoid the grassburrs, sometimes on getting an early start we would go around by the Gulf beach which was quite a distance out of our way. In taking this route though, I would generally be late at school, for there were so many little things to detain me—such as trying to catch the shadow of a flying sea gull, or trying to lasso sand crabs on my stick horse.

Crowds of Cow Boys used to come over to the Peninsula from the mainland and sometimes have occasion to rope wild steers in my presence—hence me trying to imitate them.

I remember getting into a scrape once by taking the beach route to school; sister who was a year older than I, was walking along the water edge picking up pretty shells while I was riding along on my stick horse taking the kinks out of my rope—a piece of fishline—so as to be ready to take in the first crab that showed himself. Those crabs went in large droves and sometimes ventured quite a distance out from the Gulf, but on seeing a person would break for the water.

It was not long before I spied a large drove on ahead, pulling their freight for the water. I put spurs to my pony and dashed after them. I managed to get one old fat fellow headed off and turned towards the prairie. I threw at him several times but he would always go through the loop before I could pull it up. He finally struck a hole and disappeared.

I was determined to get him out and take another whirl at him, so dropping my horse and getting down on all fours I began digging the sand away with my hands, dog fashion.

About that time sister came up and told me to come on as I would be late at school, etc.

I think I told her to please go to Halifax, as I was going to rope that crab before I quit or or "bust." At any rate she went off, leaving me digging with all my might.

Every now and then I would play dog by sticking my snoot down in the hole to smell. But I rammed it down once too often. Mr. Crab was nearer the surface than I thought for. He was laying for me. I gave a comanche yell, jumped ten feet in the air and lit out for home at a 2:40 gait. One of his claws was fastened to my upper lip while the other clamped my nose with an ironlike grip.

I met Mr. William Berge coming out to the beach after a load of wood, and he relieved me of my uncomfortable burden. He had to break the crabs claws off to get him loose.

I arrived at school just as Mr. Hale was ringing the bell after recess. He called me up and wanted to know what was the matter with my face, it was so bloody. Being a little George W., minus the hatchet, I told him the truth. Suffice to say he laid me across his knee and made me think a nest of bumble bees were having a dance in the seat of my breeches—or at least where the seat should have been. I never had a pair of pants on up to that time. Had worn nothing but a long white shirt made of a flour sack after some of the "big bugs" in Matagorda had eaten the flour out.

The fall of 1861 Mr. Hale broke up school and left for Yankeedom to join the blue coats. And from that time on I had a regular picnic, doing nothing and studying mischief. Billy Williams was my particular chum; we were constantly together doing some kind of devilment. The old women used to say we were the meanest little imps in the Settlement, and that we would be hung before we were twenty-one. Our three favorite passtimes were, riding the milk calves, coon hunting and sailing playboats down on the bay shore.

Shortly after school broke up I wore my first pair of breeches. Uncle "Nick" and aunt "Mary," mother's brother and sister, who lived in Galveston, sent us a trunk full of clothes and among them was a pair of white canvas breeches for me.

The first Sunday after the goods arrived mother made me scour myself all over and try my new pants. on. They were large enough for two kids of my size, but mother said I could wear them that day if I would be a good boy, and that she would take a few tucks in them before the next Sunday. So after getting me fixed up she told me not to leave the yard or she would skin me alive, etc.

Of course I should have been proud of the new addition to my wardrobe and like a good little boy obeyed my mother; but I wasn't a good little boy and besides the glory of wearing white pants was insignificant compared to that of an exciting coon hunt with dogs through brush, bramble and rushes. You see I had promised Billy the evening before to go coon hunting with him that day.

I watched my chance and while mother was dressing sister in her new frock I tiptoed out of the house and skipped.

Billy was waiting for me with the four dogs and off we went for the Bay shore.

Arriving there the dogs disappeared in the tall rushes barking at every jump; we jumped right in after them, up to our waists in the mud. We had a genuine good all-day coon hunt, killing several coons and one wild cat.

We gave up the hunt about sundown, and I started for home, the glory of my new pants having departed. I was indeed a sorry looking sight, covered with mud from head to foot.

I entered the house with some fear and trembling, and well I might, for mother was "laying" for me with the old black strap. The result was I slept sound that night, but couldn't sit down without pain for a week afterwards.

It was mother's wash day and I had to carry wood from the Gulf beach to keep the "pot boiling."

I tried to play off sick that morning but it would not work, for mother had noticed that I got away with two plates of mush besides three hard boiled eggs for breakfast.

Before starting out after my first load of wood, I hid the big old strap which hung by the door, for I felt it in my bones there was war in the air. I always did have a tough time of it on wash days, and I knew this Monday would bring the same old story.

At last mother got the fire started under the wash-pot which stood out in the yard and told me for about the twentieth time to go after an armful of wood. I hesitated, in hopes that she would take a notion to go herself, but when she stamped her foot and picked up a barrel stave I knew I had better be going, for when she got her Irish blood up it was dangerous to linger.

When I got out among the drift wood on the beach, I treed a cotton-tail rabbit up a hollow log, and I made up my mind to get Mr. cotton-tail out, wood or no wood.

I began digging the sand away from the log as fast as I could so as to be able to roll it down into the Gulf and drown the rabbit out.

It was a very hot day and digging the heavy sand with only my hands and a stick was slow, tiresome work. The result was I fell asleep with my head under the log and my bare legs sticking out in the hot June sun. I dreamt I died and went to a dreadful hot country and Satan was there piling hot coals on me.

Finally the sun went under a cloud, or at least I suppose it did, for the burning pain left me and I began to dream of Heaven; I thought the Lord was there sitting upon His throne of gold in the midst of scores of happy children. Calling me up to him he pointed to a large pile of fence rails down in a beautiful valley and said: "my boy you go down and carry every one of those rails up here to me before you stop."

His words landed up against my happy thoughts like a thunderbolt from a clear sky. I had been thinking of what a picnic I would have with the other children.

A walk of about one mile brought me to the pile of rails; there were more in the pile than I could count, I shouldered one of the lightest and struck out up the steep hill, thinking how I would like to be back with mother, even if I had to carry an armful of wood from the beach now and then.

When about half way up the hill I heard a terrible noise such as I had never heard before, it awakened me, and in trying to jump up I bumped my head against the log, and also filled my eyes full of sand.

When I got onto my feet and the sand out of my eyes, I discovered the whole beach, east of me, thronged with men carrying guns, and marching right towards me. The head ones were not over a hundred yards off, beating drums and blowing their horns.

It is needless to say I was scared and that I ran as fast as my legs could carry me, looking back every minute to see if they were after me. It was in this way that I ran or sprang right into the midst of Mrs. Zipprian's drove of geese, before I knew it. There were several old ganders in the drove which used to chase me every chance they got. I generally took particular pains to go around them; but this time my mind was in a different channel from what it had ever been in before, hence my not looking out for them.

As I flew past, two of the old ganders made a dive at me, but only one succeeded in catching on; he grabbed the tail of my shirt, which stuck straight out behind, in his mouth and hung on with blood in his eyes. My speed seemed to increase instead of slacken, every time the old gander would bounce up and come down, his claws would rake the skin from the calves of my legs. His death-like grip finally broke loose and I felt considerable lighter. My mind also, felt somewhat relieved.

Mother was out in the yard washing, she had picked up chips enough to boil the water; the tub was sitting upon a box and she was rubbing away with all her might, her back towards me. As I was looking over my shoulder I ran against her, knocking her, tub and all over in a pile, myself with them.

Mother got up first with her right hand in my shirt collar, I plead manfully and tried to tell her about the scores of men, but she was too mad to listen, she dragged me to where the big black strap should have hung, I knew she couldn't find it, therefore hoped to get off with a few slaps, but alas, no, she spied the mush stick and the way she gave it to me with that was a caution!

The crowd I saw proved to be Dr. Pierceson's company of rebels, who had been sent over from Matagorda to drill and be ready to fight the bluecoats when they came. It was then the summer of 1862. They located their camp on the beach, about a mile from our house, and I used to march with them all day long sometimes. The captain, Dr. Pierceson, gave me an umbrella stick which I used for a gun.

The coming fall about five thousand Yankees landed at Deckrows Point on the Peninsula and marched by our ranch on their way to the rebel camp which was stationed forty miles above, at the mouth of Caney Creek.

They camped one night close to our house and filled me up with hard-tack, which was quite a treat to a fellow living on mush and milk.

They had a five or six day fight with the rebels, neither of them coming off victorious. We could hear the guns plainly from the "Settlement." Many dead men were washed ashore on the beach. My sister and I stumbled onto one poor fellow one day, shot through the heart. His clothes were gone and his wrist was marked "J. T." in India ink.

After the battle the Yankees marched back to Deckrows Point where they remained to the end of the war; the rebels still held their ground at the mouth of Caney. Every now and then a squad from each side would meet at the "Settlement" and have a skirmish. I remember once after one of those skirmishes a crowd of Yankees rounded Mr. Williams up on the prairie—Billy and I being with him—and throwing their pistols in his face told him if they ever found him so far from home again they would kill him.

Their threats didn't scare Mr. Williams the least bit, for he afterwards slipped into their camp after dark and stole eleven head of their best horses and gave them to the rebels. But on his way back from the rebel camp, where he went to take the horses they caught him and took him aboard of a Yankee man-of-war to hang him. They had the rope around his neck ready to swing him when the General turned him loose, on account of his old age and bravery, telling him never to be caught from home again.

Fighting was going on nearly every day in sight of us; sometimes the Yankee gun boats would get into the Bay among the rebel boats, and at other times they would fight across the narrow strip of land, shooting right over the houses at one another. Many of the cannon balls dropped on the prairie; one of them at one time struck within a few feet of Mr. Williams, almost burying him in the sand as it plowed along on the ground. Poor fellow, he was afterwards killed by one, he carried one home and taking all the powder out of it, as he supposed, set it out in the yard with the hole up, and then told Billy to get him a coal of fire in the tongs. He thought it would just flash a little.

I was present, and not liking the looks of it, crept out behind the picket gate, a few yards away, and peeped between the pickets.

The whole family was looking on to see the fun, Mattie, one of the little girls, was sitting with her arms around a dog's neck, within a few feet of it.

Billy, arriving with the coal, handed it to his father who reached over and let it drop down into the hole—where he had taken out the lead screw.

It seemed to me that the coal hadn't reached the hole when the thing exploded. For a few seconds everything was enveloped in smoke; when the smoke disappeared sufficiently for me to see, the whole sky seemed to be a blaze of fire, and finally Mr. Williams emerged out of the heavy cloud of smoke hopping on one leg.

A piece of the bomb-shell had taken off part of one foot on the left leg and another piece had plowed through the calf of his right leg; part of one ear was also gone. He only lived a few days.

A piece of the shell took off one of the dog's legs without even touching Mattie, the little girl who had her arms around his neck.

Several pieces went through the house, and one piece went through the picket gate right over my head. The next day Billy and I found a large piece sticking in the wall of an old vacant house a mile from where it exploded.

During the war several ships were driven ashore on the beach by the Yankee gun boats. The folks at the "Settlement" would get all the plunder. One ship was loaded with dry goods and from that time on I wore breeches.

About a year after the war broke out the rebels gathered up all the cattle on the Peninsula and drove them to the mainland, where they were turned loose with the thousands upon thousands of wild cattle already over there. Their idea in doing so was to keep the

Yankees—whom they knew would hold the lower part of the Peninsula, they having the best gunboats—from getting fresh beef to eat. There was only one cow left in the whole "Settlement" and that was our old "Browny;" mother had begged manfully for them to leave her, for she knew we children would starve to death living on mush straight.

When the war broke up everybody was happy. We cheered for joy when Mr. Joe Yeamans brought the good news from town.

Shortly after this all of the men and boys that were large enough, went over to the mainland to gather up the Peninsula cattle. On their arrival they found it a bigger job than they had figured on, for they were scattered over two or three hundred miles of country and as wild as deer.

Billy and I thought it very hard that we could not go and be Cow Boys too; but we had lots of fun all by ourselves, for we had an old mule and two or three ponies to ride, so you see we practiced riding in anticipation of the near future, when we would be large enough to be Cow Boys.

After being gone about three months the crowd came back, bringing with them several hundred head of cattle, which they had succeeded in gathering. Among them were about twenty head belonging to mother.

The crowd went right back after more. This stimulated Billy and I to become a crowd of Cow Boys all by ourselves, therefore we put in most of our time lassoing and riding wild yearlings, etc. We hardly stayed at home long enough to get our meals. Mother had to get her own wood in those days, for sister had gone to school in Galveston. Of course I always had to come home at night, therefore mother would get satisfaction out of me with the black strap or mush stick, after I was snugly settled in bed, for my waywardness and trifling habits.

In the spring of 1867, a cattle man by the name of Faldien brought his family over to the Peninsula for their health and rented part of our house to live in.

After getting his wife and babies located in their new quarters, he started back home, to Matagorda, to make preparations for spring work, he having to rig up new outfits, etc. He persuaded mother to let me go with him, and learn to run cattle. When she consented I was the happiest boy in the "Settlement," for my life long wish was about to be gratified.

Frontier Girlhood

In the following passage Malinda Jenkins, a mid-western farm girl, describes her childhood. (Jesse Lilienthal, ed., Gambler's Wife, *3-12.)*

My mother's maiden name was Goben. I was only five years old when she died. It must have been in 1853, as I was born in 1848. If mother had lived I would have known her people, too, but as it was I never knew none of them except her brother, Uncle Jess Goben, that was a preacher. I don't know what denomination he belonged to but they preached that everybody is saved and nobody goes to hell—perdition they called it.

Betty used to tell me how they cut down the trees and built the house that the rest of us was born in. They tied a small cow-bell on Betty's neck to keep track of her. But she would hold the clapper so's she could play and go where she wanted. Another baby had come and they wanted Betty to stay close and sometimes rock the cradle. But Betty wanted to play.

The second child was Nancy. Susan was the next, and after Susan come Mary and brother Alfred. Then Abram and James but they died young. Then me. William Thomas Jefferson was the youngest. People had families them days.

The only thing that was wrong with us was too much religion. The whole family was that way, the cousins and the rest of them; ministers galore and religion crazy. My brother-in-law was a preacher, and my cousin was the famous Abram Plunkett of the Christian Church in Indiana.

I was religious too, until I found out you couldn't pray for things—that you had to work for them to get what you wanted. . . . I was the wild one, if you could call me that, because I left the old homestead and pulled out. Left behind everything, all their prayers and old beliefs, and went out and learned something. That's just what I done. I had no education in school but books ain't everything, seeing and remembering is important, too.

All my people and the things I seen in my early days didn't count for long. They passed by and was gone. Mostly you live and die with them you growed up with. Not me. I cleared out too young.

The family made everything that could be made at home. When anything come from a store it was because there wasn't no other way to get it. My sisters was spinning and weaving half the time.

The spinning wheel and hand loom stood in the kitchen. That was a separate house, about eighteen by twenty foot in size. It was a big one for them parts, with a chimney and fireplace, and the regulation crane and kettle to heat the water in. Twelve foot away stood another house of the same size, that we lived in. Both of them was log houses. They was cold and full of cracks and took a deal of heating.

I remember one fall day. I don't suppose I was much over three years old. Susan was weaving on the big loom over by the window. Mary set at the spinning wheel on the other side of the room, making thread out of wool rolls. There wasn't no dinner cooked that day, everybody was out except my two sisters and me.

I was begging for something to eat. 'Let's feed her,' one of them said, 'and when she gets enough maybe she'll let us alone and we can have a little quiet.' They told me they had the fireplace full of potatoes, roasting under the coals. After a while they set them in a pan outside by the kitchen door where the salt gourd stood.

I et potatoes—and salt by the handful. That night I had a regular spasm. I guess it was the salt that done it. The whole family was scared. They kept passing me around the room from one to another. First one took me, trying to do for me, and then the next.

Something was in my mouth I was trying to get shut of, see. A spoon handle to keep me from chewing my tongue. They put salt on my tongue too, the very thing that had made me sick! But salt was all they knowed to break a spasm. Me fighting them all, and them passing me around with the salt gourd chasing after me. At last I was so sick I spewed up over everything and everybody. . . . I must have fell asleep then. When I woke up later I was in my little trundle bed and somebody was setting by me. For awhile they thought it was all over with Linney. From that day to this, and it's eighty years ago, I ain't et a potato with a speck of salt on it.

My brothers and sisters strung along at all ages. Some of them was growed up and married when I was just a little kid. My sister Betty's first was named Jeby. When she was four years old I was only five. Jeby was the biggest coward, but I loved her best in all the world. That didn't keep me from trying to scare her in all sorts of ways. As for me, I wasn't scared of nothing. Not then. But later on in life I knowed what it was to be scared of things, too. You get wiser as you grow older, and the wiser you get the more scary and careful you are.

Brother Alfred was growed up. He come riding down the road toward the house, one day, and as he got nearer I could see that something was lying, like a sack of meal, across the horse's neck. It was my little brother Abram, about four years older than me. Mother run out and lifted Abram off the horse. He was deathly sick, all white and pale. Abram was her favorite of us all.

He was hot with fever, I reckon, for she was putting cold water on his head. She told me to run to the spring with the gourd and fill it. It was only twenty yards off but like a bad child I didn't want to do it.

She had to tell me twice. I didn't want no water; I didn't see why I should go. I went but I brought it sulky.

Five days more and Abram was dead of typhoid. Then I got my punishment. Young as I was I wet my pillow with tears because I didn't fetch that water right off. . . . I done a wrong act—it seemed to me to be very serious and I never could forget it. You can't lie to your conscience when it comes to a thing like that; you can't make the wrong look right.

Next day—he was still lying there in the house—I was looking around for mother. I found her outside on her knees with her hands lifted before her face and praying: 'Oh sweet Jesus, take my little darlin' into your arms.'

Then I happened to look up and I seen a man dressed in white and I thought it was an angel coming! I let out a yelp and run for the house. We had one of them old-fashioned foot-boards with the draperies hanging down to hide the trundle bed underneath. Mother had to pull me out from under it; I thought the angel had come to take us all.

It wasn't an angel, but Mr. Gelty, a friend, that come to see if he could help. It was right in the middle of summer, terrible hot, and he was dressed in homemade linen. Them Geltys was queer folk—strait-laced even for then. The daughters looked it; one of them said that a woman that read a newspaper wasn't fit to be a wife. I wish she could see some of the young gals around here today.

Mother put in a month praying and grieving for her child. Then she took down, her and little Jeby. I don't remember nothing that happened until one night Uncle John Dean waked me up. He took me out of mother's bed. I was cold and all crumpled up. I reckon I was right sleepy.

Come sun up. When I set up in bed I seen a long white sheet, spread over a board, on two chairs about six foot apart. Mother had died in the night. Across over to the door, on the opposite side of the room, was another sheet and two chairs but something much shorter.

I run to papa's bed and shook him. He wasn't asleep, he just had his eyes shut.

'Daddy, daddy, what are them things?' I was crying already.

'Don't cry,' he said, and put his hands on my shoulders and patted me. 'She's left us and went to a better place. . . .'

'But how can we do without her?'

'We have to. I'll take care of you and be good to you like always.'

I asked him, 'Who is the other one?'

'It's Jeby.'

We had three deaths in the family in about a month.

It wasn't more than a week and papa had the typhoid. My sister Susan took him over to her house, and my little brother Tommy. They moved papa in a wagon, on a mattress.

Papa got over it all right. Meanwhile Tommy—we called him Buddy, his name, was Thomas Jefferson—took down with it. He got over it, too.

Buddy just commenced to walk. He had to learn it all over after the sickness. Not long afterward he was outside when somebody come along on a horse to talk to Susan's husband, Albert Fields, the shoe-maker preacher. The man tied his horse to a locust bush in

front of the house. It got tangled up in its bridle and fell. Buddy run
in as fast as he could and hollered, 'Mister, your horse is chokin!'

They got the bridle off but the horse couldn't get up at first. It was
a close call, Buddy was right. The man said, 'Well son, you sure
saved my horse.' He turned to Albert, 'You make him a pair of shoes
and I'll pay the damage.'

But Buddy piped up: 'I don't want no shoes, I wants a pair of
boots with red tops!' They had a big laugh over that. Albert made
him a beautiful pair which the man paid for. . . . In them days you
couldn't give a little boy nothing in the world that would please him
so much as a pair of red top boots.

Papa called me Sinney, little Sinney. He got that from Linney that
everybody else called me. Malinda was my mother's name. I was
named after her.

When my mother was dying she asked papa to let sister Mary take
and raise me. Mary was the only one of the girls that had married
pretty well off and had a good home of her own. But papa kept me
until he married again a year later. Then he took me to Mary the way
mother wanted.

I was very happy there but papa wouldn't let me stay. He missed
me and wanted me back, but I was too little to understand how that
could be. I knew that he was married to a woman I didn't know, and
I wanted to stay where I was.

My stepmother was Mary Huffman. She had been a widow for
years. The thing I remember best about her was her sewing; she was
a fine seamstress. Children don't like stepmothers, as a rule, but I
thought the world of Mary Huffman. She had her peculiarities but
never was a better stepmother, I guess, that ever lived. I loved her
truly; we all did.

So Papa come and took me away from my sister Mary's. I went
kicking and screaming. I was a red-head kid with a temper. When he
got me home I wouldn't eat, and I wouldn't go to bed. They left me
alone to see what I would do. I set by the fire and slept there with my
head up against the jamb of the fireplace. I never left it, only for the
seconds when I had to. I stayed there two days and nights crying
myself to sleep.

The third day I heard papa say, 'I can't stand this, I can't see Sinney cryin' and unhappy. I can't stand no more of it; it's best to take

her back to Mary's. When she gets ready to come home it will be time enough.' That day they took me back. It was kind of like the hunger strikes you hear of these days.

A year later they sent my little brother to fetch me home to go to school. When I got there they asked me a thousand questions about Mary's house, and how she lived, and so on. You see, she was better off than us, and they was curious. I didn't like that but I told them everything I knew. They wasn't satisfied; they kept asking me more questions. Not papa, but Alfred wouldn't let me alone.

The first thing I noticed to home was an old umbrella. It's hard to believe, but up to that time—and I was seven years old—I hadn't never seen one. I was always playing with it, opening it and trying to make the wind lift me off the ground. I played this way with Tiny Owens, another little girl that got hold of a second umbrella over to her place.

So one day I told them how me and Tiny was up to the hay loft and opened our umbrellas and jumped out. And that the wind carried us away off, and a farm hand come running up to see if we was hurt, and we said no, that everything was fine.

I knew that was a whopper of a lie but I don't know to this day why I told it, only that Alfred had been pestering me some more and I was mad. Maybe that was the reason, or maybe not. When children tell lies I think they just sort of come out.

I said to myself, 'It's a lie but I don't believe they will ever find it out.' I worried about it a lot though.

Papa spoke about it when he come in and I heard him. It frightened me terrible. 'Sinney's a good child and don't seem to be the lyin' sort but there's something about it I don't understand at all.'

Alfred just said, 'It's a lie!'

It didn't seem like I slept much that night. Papa catched on to it mighty quick, I thought. I was pretty sick over it.

Next morning I heard him say to my stepmother: 'She never told me a lie and I can't believe she'd make up a bald-face one like that without a reason. Maybe the child dreamed it.'

Oh what glory, the child dreamed it! When papa said that I knew I was saved. And I was cured from lying. It made me fearful of a lie and was one of the best things that ever happened to me. I don't like to think about it even today. I hate lying and I hate liars.

I was going on eight when they started me off to school—with a psalm book. It has big letters on the outside edge in the song, commencing with A and going right down to Z.

Well now, in the first place, there's a streak of pride in me that I can't and never could subdue. It crops up. I am proud. I can't bear nothing that ain't the way it should be and I knew it wasn't right for me to use a psalm book for me A.B.C's.

I cried nearly all the way to school. The other children had spelling books, and McGuffey's First Reader and Second Reader, and all that. I had nothing but my old song book, and I was terribly ashamed of it.

I had two stepbrothers that was going to school with me and Buddy. Buddy was big enough to go along, so I was pretty old to start in. Maybe I wouldn't have been so humiliated if I hadn't been that old.

This here stepbrother of mine, the biggest of the two, was named Drury Staton. We called him Drew. His brother Joe was cross-eyed and homely but an awful good boy. Drew was all right enough but a glutton. He'd eat up every mouthful of his lunch and most of ours before we ever got to school. Just think of that. In the morning, right after breakfast, he'd eat up the lunch. It didn't matter which was going to carry the lunch, Drew took it away. So we got in the habit of eating, too, to keep him from getting it all.

That was my start in school. The boys went out to play—they didn't care so much—but I had to set there with the girls at recess, watching them eat lunch and me with nothing.

I have thought of it many times since—I used to pray to die to keep from having to go to school. With the wrong schoolbook and no lunch. I begged so hard to keep from going that my stepmother interfered. 'If she don't want to go to school let her stay home and learn herself,' she told papa. 'Alfred's advanced, he can learn her.'

Alfred had a good education. All of them had—but me. Alfred taught school later, and my sister Betty was a practicing doctor.

When papa said, 'All right, you don't have to go no more,' I hugged and kissed him. I couldn't have stood it much longer without running away.

Gold Camp School

*On the farthest edge of the frontier, education was often of the
most rudimentary sort. Prentice Mulford, who followed the lure of
gold to California, took to teaching to stay alive when his expectations of riches proved illusory.* (Prentice Mulford's Story: Life by
Land and Sea, *New York, 1889, 145-50.)*

I was not confident of my ability to teach even a "common
school" when the situation was offered me in a little Tuolumne
County mining camp. I said so to my old friend, Pete H., who had
secured me the position. "Well," said he, after a reflective pause, "do
you retain a clear recollection of twenty-six letters of the alphabet?
For if you do, you are equal to any educational demand this camp
will make on you."

It was a reckless "camp." No phase of life was viewed or treated
seriously. They did walk their horses to the grave slowly at a funeral,
but how they did race back! It was legally necessary, however, that I
should be examined as to my ability by the school trustees. These
were Dr. D., Bill K., a saloon-keeper, and Tom J., a miner. I met
them in the Justice's office. The doctor was an important appearing
man, rotund, pompous, well-dressed, and spectacled. He glared at
me with an expression betwixt sadness and severity. I saw he was to
be the chief inquisitor. I expected from him a searching examination,
and trembled. It was years since I had seen a school-book. I knew
that in geography I was rusty and in mathematics musty.

Before the doctor lay one thin book. It turned out to be a spelling
book. The doctor opened it, glared on me leisurely, and finally said:
"Spell cat." I did so. "Spell hat." I spelled. "Rat," said the doctor,
with a look of explosive fierceness and in a tone an octave higher. I
spelled, and then remarked: "But, doctor, you surely must know that
I can spell words of one syllable?" "I don't," he shouted, and pro-
pounded "mat" for me to spell, with an increase of energy in his
voice, and so went on until I had so spelled long enough to amuse
him and the other two trustee triflers. Then he shut the book, saying:
"Young man, you'll do for our camp. I wouldn't teach that school
for $5,000 a year; and there are two boys you'll have for scholars

that I advise you to kill, if possible, the first week. Let's all go over and take a drink.''

My school house was the church, built and paid for partly by the gamblers and partly by the good people of Jimtown "for the use of all sects'' on Sundays, and for educational purposes on week days.

I was shut up in that little church six hours a day with sixty children and youths, ranging from four to eighteen years of age. In summer it was a fiercely hot little church. The mercury was always near 90 by noon, and sometimes over 100, and you could at times hear shingles split and crack on the roof of the cathedral. A few years of interior California summers' suns will turn unpainted boards and shingles almost as black as charcoal.

The majority of my pupils' parents being from New England and North America, they brought and carried into effect all their North American ideas of education. The California summer heat is, I think, unfit for educational purposes. It is too hot to herd sixty restless children together six hours a day. They proved this in several cases. Some fell sick suddenly. Some fainted. But this made no difference. The school went on in all its misery. I sent a fainting child home one day, and the father returned with it an hour afterward. He was fierce, and said he wanted his child kept in school when he sent it to school.

This was in California's early days. My scholars were the children of the Argonauts, and in some cases had come out with them. There was then no regular system of text-books. Publishers had not commenced making fortunes by getting out a new school-book system every three years.

My scholars came bringing a great variety of school-books. They brought "Pike's Arithmetic,'' which had come over the plains, and "Smith's Geography,'' which had sailed around Cape Horn. Seldom were two alike. But the greatest variety lay in grammars. There was a regular museum of English grammars, whose authors fought each other with different rules and called the various parts of speech by different names. I accounted for the great variety of grammars on the supposition that it is or was the ambition of a large proportion of schoolmasters to write a work on grammar before they died and say: "I have left another grammar to bless and confuse posterity.''

Besides bringing grammars, most of the boys brought dogs. Dogs of many breeds and sizes hovered around the school-house. They wanted frequently to come in, and did often come in, to sneak under the seats and lay themselves at their masters' feet. I had frequently to kick or order them out, and I noticed that whenever a dog was chased he would take the longest road to get out and under as many seats as possible, in order to receive as many kicks as possible from the youthful owners of the other dogs.

I could not so organize a battalion of ten different grammars as to act in concert on my grammar class of twenty pupils. So I put them all on the retired list and tried to teach this so-called "science" orally. I chalked the rules on the blackboard, as well as the names of the different parts of speech. I made my scholars commit these to memory, standing, although I will not argue that memory takes any stronger grip on a thing while the pupil stands. At last I taught a few with good memories to "parse." I worked hard with that grammar class, and was very proud of their proficiency until I found that after months of this drilling they neither spoke nor wrote any better English than before. However, I lost nothing by this experience, for it helped me to the conviction I have held to ever since, that the entire grammar system and method does very little to make one habitually use correct language, and that a taste for reading and constant association with correct English-speaking people does a great deal. As for spending time in "parsing," I think it would be better to use that force in learning the boy to shoe horses and the girl to make bread, or let the girl shoe the horses if she wants to and the boy make the bread.

The labor of teaching the alphabet to ten infants, calling them up once an hour "to say their letters," is, in my estimation, greater than that of swinging a pick in the surface gold "diggings." I have tried both, and infinitely prefer the pick. It is not so much work when you are employed with them as when you are occupied with the other pupils. Then these poor little alphabetical cherubs can do nothing but squirm on their low benches, catch flies, pinch each other, make and project spit-balls and hold up their hands for another drink of water. I could not let them out of doors to play in the sand, where they should have been, because the North American parent would have considered himself as defrauded of a part of his infant's schooling were they not imprisoned the whole six hours.

Neither can you set a child to studying A or M or any other letter.

There is not an idea in A or B. During the two years of my administration I wrought with one child who never could get successfully beyond F. Her parents questioned my ability as a teacher. Some days she would repeat the whole alphabet correctly. I would go home with a load off my mind. The next day her mind would relapse into an alphabetical blank after F. She grew to be an eyesore to me. The sight of her at last made me sick.

I held public examinations every six months, and was careful to do all the examining myself. An interloper among the audience I invited did me great damage on one of these memorized performances by asking a simple arithmetical question of the show-off geograpical boy. The urchin was brilliant in dealing with boundary lines, capes, and islands, but his head was one that mathematics could not readily be injected into. On the other hand, my specimen grammarian was as likely to describe an island as a body of land surrounded-by land as by water. I had no heart to find fault with this poor barefooted urchin who, when in class, was always trying to stand on one leg like a crane, and sending his right big toe on exploring scratching expeditions up his left trouser. He had been born and brought up in an inland country, where no body of water was to be seen save an occasional fleeting mud puddle; and what earthly conception could he form of the ocean and its islands?

But the parents who attended these exhibitions of stuffed memories were struck at the proficiency of the progeny, and retired with the impression that their children knew a great deal because they had parroted off so much that was all Greek to them; and after I had been in this occupation a year I would sit in my empty theological school-house when they had gone and try and convict myself as a profound humbug, and one, too, compelled, in order to get a living, to encourage and foster a system which had so much humbug in it.

The California schools were not then "graded." They were conducted on the "go-as-you-please" plan, sometimes going as the teachers pleased, sometimes as the parents pleased, sometimes as the pupils pleased. The parents of the youthful brains I was trying to develop into future statesmen and presidents wanted me to teach many things. One father wished his son taught Latin. It is bringing extremes pretty near each other to teach Latin and A B C's. But I "taught" the young man Latin as I was "taught" many things at school. I started him committing to memory the Latin declensions and conjugations, and then heard him "say his lesson." If he got anything out of it I didn't know what it was, except tough work. He never reached any translations of the classics, for several reasons.

Higher (?) Education

In 1824 Bayard Rush Hall, a Presbyterian clergyman and graduate of Princeton, became the first principal of Indiana State Seminary, a school which grew into the state university. His problems were typical of hundreds of pioneering educational efforts to follow. In the following autobiographical passage he recounts the early period, calling himself Charles Clarence. (B. R. Hall, The New Purchase, *New York, (1843), II, 77-78, 80-86.)*

Our fourth year introduces an epoch, the Augustan age of the New Purchase—the opening of the State College!

And now comes on the stage, as one principal actor, my friend, the Reverend Charles Clarence, A.M., Principal and Professor of Ancient Languages. This gentleman had accepted our appointment, not for the paltry stipend paid as his salary, but wholly because he longed to be in the romantic West, and among its earliest literary pioneers; and hence, early this spring, he was with us, and not merely ready, but even enthusiastically impatient to commence his labours. . . .

Here was a sad waking from day-dreaming! and Clarence was with us, having altered views of life, and seeing that we have something to do in it, besides to amuse or be amused. Happy chastisement our friend afterwards deemed it, when encountering sore disappointments and many, in his professional career: ay! he was destined to endure the utter crushing of all his high hopes and purposes. For, if ever man was influenced by disinterested motives, and fired with enthusiasm for advancing solid learning,—if ever one desirous of seeing Western institutions rival if not excel others,—if ever a person came willing to live and die with us, and to sacrifice eastern tastes and prejudices, and become, in every proper way, a Western Man, my friend Clarence was he.

His labours and actions proved this. Look for instance at his daily teaching—his five and six hours usually spent in the recitation room; at his preaching, always twice on the Sabbath, and commonly several times during the week; at his visits to the sick and the dying, and his attendance on funerals! And these things extended beyond his own denomination—when requested, and that was often; for rarely, even in his own sicknesses and melancholy hours, did he refuse what seemed his duty to others. When too feeble to leave his house, he heard the recitations in his bed; and when unable to stand, he sat in his congregation and preached, his person emaciated and his face death-like. Nor did he confine his teaching to the routine himself had followed, but he introduced other branches, and also a course of Greek, unknown then in western colleges, and not common in eastern ones; and this, although it added to the severity of his private studies, and for many months kept his lamp burning even till two o'clock! His only inquiry was, how can I best promote the interests of the institution? In short, therefore, all his learning, his talents, his experience, his accomplishments, were freely and heartily employed and given, in season and out of season;—and a knowledge of all the music he possessed, vocal and instrumental, was imparted, *gratuitously,* to the students—and also grammar, moral philosophy, and the like, *gratuitously* and at *extra* hours, to certain teachers of ordinary schools, and some of these his former opponents! . . .

Be it remembered, as was intimated in the early part of volume first, that Uncle Sam is an undoubted friend of *public* education, and that, although so sadly deficient in his own; and hence, in the liberal distribution of other folk's land, he bestowed on us several entire townships for a college or university. It was, therefore, democratically believed, and loudly insisted on, that as the State had freely received, it should freely give; and that "larnin, even the most powerfullest highest larnin," should at once be bestowed on every body! and without a farthing's expense! Indeed, some gravely said and argued that teachers and professors in the "people's college ought to starve for the honour!" or at least be content with "a dollar a day, which was more nor double what a feller got for mauling rails!" The popular wrath therefore was at once excited almost to fury when necessity compelled us to fix our tuition fee at ten dollars a year; and the greatest indignation was felt and expressed towards Clarence "as the feller what tuk hire for teaching and preaching, and was gettin to be a big-bug on the poor people's edicashin money.''

Be it recollected too, that both big and little colleges were erected by persons who, with reverence be it spoken, in all matters pertaining to ''high larnin,'' had not sufficient discrimination to know the second letter of an alphabet from a buffalo's foot. Nothing, we incline to believe, can ever make State schools and colleges very good ones; but nothing can make them *so* bad, we repeat, as for Uncle Sam to leave every point open to debate, especially among ignorant, prejudiced, and selfish folks in a New Purchase. For while trustees may be ninnies, nincompoops, or even ninnyhammers as to proper plans and buildings, yet are such when masons, bricklayers and carpenters, keen-sighted enough to secure the building contracts for themselves and their friends, and curiously exorbitant in their demands on the sub-treasurers for their silly work. The mean-looking and ridiculous arrangements at Woodville cost as much, perhaps more, than *suitable* things would have cost; so that when a college is to be commenced it ought to be done, not only by wise, learned, classical men; but as such are not abundant in very new settlements, let such men at Washington—(and such *are* at Uncle Sam's bureau)—let them prescribe when, and how, and where, our new western institutions are to be; and if rebellious democrats refuse the gift so encumbered, let it thus be given to more modest and quiet democrats.

Proceed we, however, to open the college. And my narration may be depended on, as Clarence had reviewed the whole and says it is substantially correct,—indeed, in some respect I was a *quorum-pars*.

The institution was opened the first day of May, at 9-1/2 o'clock, A.M., anno Domini 1800 and so forth. And, some floors being unlaid, and the sashes all being without glass, the opening was as complete as possible—nearly like that of an Irish hedge school! When the Principal—(so named in our minutes and papers, but by the vulgar called *master*, and by the middle sort, *teacher*,) appeared, a clever sprinkle of *boy* was in waiting; most of which firmly believed that, by some magic art, our hero *could*, and being paid by government, *should*, and without putting any body to the expense of books and implements, touch and transmute all, and in less than no time, into great scholars.

''Boys and *young gentlemen*,'' said Mr. C. compounding the styles of a pedagogue and professor, ''I am happy to see you; and we are now about to commence our State College, or, as some call it, the Seminary. I hope all feel what an honour attends being the first students in an institution so well endowed; and which, therefore, by proper exertions on our parts, may eventually rise to the level of eastern colleges, and become a blessing to our State and country. You have all, I suppose, procured the necessary books, of which notice was given at meeting, and in several other ways, for the last four weeks.''

''I've got 'em—''

''Me too—''

''I've brung most on 'em—''

''Master—Uncle Billy's to fetch mine out in his wagon about Monday next—''

''Father says he couldn't mind the names and wants them on a paper—''

''Books!—I never heern tell of any books—wont these here ones do, Master?—this here's the Western Spellin one—and this one's the Western Kalkelatur?''

''Mr. Clarinse—I fotch'd my copy-book and a bottle of red-ink to sit down siferin in—and daddy wants me to larn book-keepin and surveyin.''

''Order boys—order!''—(hem!)—''let all take seats in front. There is a misunderstanding with some, both as to the books and the whole design and plan of the school, I perceive. This is a Classical and Mathematical School; and that fact is stated and fully explained in the trustees' public advertisements; and no person can be admitted unless one intending to enter upon and pursue the prescribed course; and that includes even at the start Latin, Greek, and Algebra. Now, first let us see who are to study the dead languages—''

''I do—I do—me to—me to,'' &c., &c.

''Do you, then, sit there. Well—now let me have your names for the roll—A. Berry—S. Smith—C. D. &c., &c.—ten names—I will attend to you ten directly, so soon as I have dismissed the others. I regret, my young friends, that you are disappointed—but I am only doing my duty; indeed, if I wished I have no power to admit you, unless to the course of studies—nay, even the trustees have power to do only what they have done. I hope, therefore, you will go home, and explain the matter to your friends—''

By several—

"Daddy says he doesn't see no sort a use in the high larn'd things—and he wants me to larn Inglish only, and bookkeepin, and surveyin, so as to tend store and run a line."

"I allow, Mister, we've near on about as good a right to be larn'd what we wants, as them tother fellers on that bench;—it's a free school for all."

"I am sorry, boys, for this misunderstanding; but we cannot argue the subject here. And yet every one must see one matter plainly; for instance, any man has a right to be governor, or judge, or congressman; yet none of you can be elected before the legal age, and before having some other qualifications. It is so here, you all have a right to what we have to bestow; but you must be qualified to enter; and must be content to receive the gift of the State in the way the law provides and orders. You will please go home now."

The disappointed youngsters accordingly withdrew; and with no greater rudeness than was to be expected from undisciplined chaps, full of false notions of rights, and possessed by a wild spirit of independence. Hence, Mr. C. heard some very flattering sentiments growled at him by the retiring young democrats; but which, when they had fairly reached the entry, were bawled and shouted out frankly and fearlessly. And naturally after this he was honoured with some high sounding epithets by certain hypocritical demagogues in rabble-rousing speeches—sneaking-gentlemen, who aimed to get office and power by endless slanders on the college, and most pitiful and malicious slang about "liberty and equality, and rights, and tyranny, and big-bugs, and poor people, and popular education," *et id omme genus!*

Ay! certain small-potato-patriots publicly on the stump avowed "it was a right smart chance better to have no collidge no how, if all folks hadn't equal right to larn what they most liked best." And two second-rate pettifoggers electioneered on this principle; "that it was consistent with the republicanism taught by the immortal Jefferson, and with the genius of our institutions, to use the college funds to establish common schools for rich and poor alike, and make the blessings of education like air, sunshine, and water!"

Clarence, therefore, was now hated and villified, as the supposed instrument of pride and aristocracy, in drawing a line between rich and poor; and for a while his person, his family, his very house was abominated. On one occasion he was in Woodville when a half drunken brute thus halloed against him—"Thare goes that darn'd high larn'd bug what gits nine hundred and ninety-nine dollars and ninety-nine cents of the people's eddekashin money for larnin ristekrats sons high flown words—gimme that 'are stone and I'll do for him." Whether this was fun or earnest, Clarence did not care to ascertain; for hearing the sneers and derision of the bystanders, and fearing it might become earnest, he took shelter in my store.

At another time walking with Professor Harwood in the outskirts of the village, they heard a cry in their rear—"knock 'em down"—when suddenly turning, there stood a stout chap flourishing a bludgeon over their heads, evidently, indeed, in a *sort* of fun, which was, however, an index of the popular ill-will and spite.

When persons rode by his dwelling, remarks like the following would be shouted forth:—

"Well—thar's whar the grammur man lives that larns 'em Latin and grand-like things—allow we'll oust him yet—he doesn't own little college any how; he's poor as Job's turkey, if it want for that powerful sallury the trustees give him."

Clarence's salary was four hundred dollars per annum!

"Well," bawled out one fellow—"dog my hide if that ain't the furst time I ever seed that big man's door open!—hem!—powerful fine carpet!—(a beautiful rag carpet made by Mrs. C.)—allow, people's eddekashin money *bought* that!"

Even Mr. C.'s gratuitous preaching could not secure him from ill-natured remarks. "Well," said an occasional hearer to another once —"how do y'like that sort a preachin?" "Foo!" was the reply. "I don't want no more sich! I like a man that kin jist read, and then I know it comes from the sperit! he tuk out his gold watch twice to show it, and was so d——mnation proud he wouldn't kneel down to pray!"

But the reader may wish to know how Mr. Clarence got along with "the Few." Well, as the warm weather approached, the "boys and young gentlemen" came to recitation without coats; and, as the thermometer arose, they came without *shoes* —

"What! in the State college? Could your Mr. Clarence not have things ordered with more decency?"

Softly, Mr. Dignity—in a world where our presiding judge, a man of worth and great abilities, presided in court without his coat and cravat, and with his feet modestly reposed on the upper rostrum, thus showing his boot-soles to by-standers and lawyers; where lawyers were stripped and in shirt-sleeves; and where even Governor Sunbeam, in a stump speech, gave blast to his nose pinched between a thumb and finger, and wiped said pinchers afterwards on the hinder regions of his inexpressibles; do you, sir, think our Mr. C., or all eastern dignitaries combined, could have compelled young bushwackers to wear coats and shoes in recitation rooms? He indeed ventured once as follows:—

"Young *gentlemen*"—(hem!)—"why do you attend recitations without coats and shoes?"

" 'Tis cooler, sir!"—with surprise.

"Ay! so it is—perhaps it would be still cooler if you came without your *pantaloons*."

Haw! haw!—by the whole ten.

"And *did* they, Mr. Carlton, come without their indispensables?"

Oh! dear me! no; on the contrary, the young gentlemen were so tickled at our professor's pleasant hint direct, that next day they not only come in their breeches, but also with shoes and coats on! But still, many proper regulations of our friend were distasteful to scholars and parents equally—for instance, the requirement of a written excuse for certain absences. One parent, an upper class Thompsonian doctor, did, indeed, once send a note—but that was an insolent and peremptory order to Clarence to believe in future his son, without a written excuse! And another person, a captain in the *late* war, not only refused to write a note, but he sent a verbal message by his son to the master, viz.—"Charley Clarence, you needn't think of introducing your d——n Yankee tricks out here!"

III. LOVE AND MARRIAGE

Pioneer courtship and marriage customs, sexual mores, and family organization were generally no different from those of Americans in settled regions. What made for some difference? What ''calculations'' did a girl make in choosing a husband? What are the basic differences between these pioneers' attitudes toward love and marriage and the attitudes held by Americans today? How was sex regarded?

Malinda Jenkins' Marriages
(Lilienthal, Gambler's Wife, 37-43, 78-79, 121-26.)

I took to Bill Young because I knew he had people that amounted to something—his uncle lived close by—while this other fellow, Gribben, hadn't nobody that I knew of. Don't that show how calculating a young girl can be when she ain't really in love with a man?

I got to going with Bill. What I mean is, that when the time come for bed, Bill would be asking me to sit up with him an hour or so after the others turned in. Bill was all right.

Nancy said to me, 'I think you have made your choice but I would have taken the other one. He's got more brains, he talks best and he's best lookin'.'

'I know something about Bill,' I answered, 'and I don't know nothing about Joe.'

'Bill Young says he's all right.' Bill told Nancy he thought Joe's people had plenty of money.

It went on this way for some time and I was beginning to like Bill pretty well—he was more lively than Joe. Joe Gribben was certainly a gentleman but awful serious.

In about a month Joe had a bad accident. They was cutting wood and shipping it away by the carload. Him and Bill was doing this. Joe's axe slipped and slit his foot wide open. He near bled to death before they got the doctor. They had to cord up his leg to stop the bleeding. The doctor dressed it every day for two weeks. He wanted Joe to go to the hospital in Ladoga. But no sir, Joe just stayed on.

Well, I reckon I fell in love with Joe. Bill Young was there, too. They got so's they wouldn't speak to each other hardly. Bill was always nice and courteous to me. But he told me, 'I step out—Joe's the one you are in love with.'

Joe asked me to marry him. I said I wouldn't give him his answer until I seen my dad. There's where I know now that I wasn't in love with him. Love ain't like that.

Papa and my stepmother come to visit Nancy about this time. Papa said as it was all right, he thought Joe was a gentleman. I told papa I didn't like the idea of leaving him and living in Kentucky. 'Never mind,' he said, 'you can work Joe to come and buy round these parts.'

Well sir, it sure is strange when you think about it, how scary a child can be when it comes to taking her out of her element. Joe told me he was going home to make arrangements for us to live in Lexington. 'We'll get married here, then I'm takin' you to my sister's. I want you to have a governess that'll learn you everything that is pertainin' to a lady, to take your place in life where you belong.' I began to think on that. What I had to go through with, me that had never been to school. The more I studied on it the worse afeared I got. I talked to papa and to Nancy. There wasn't nothing I'd keep from them and my stepmother.

Long after I found out that Joe's people was stylish and went in Lexington society. Joe didn't want to rush me into that without he felt I could be happy there, knowing as much as everybody else knew. He was trying to make it easy for me. He didn't want me to grieve and sicken.

He went home to fix everything while I was having time to think. And thinking about it sure enough made me sick—just what Joe didn't want to happen. I begun to get pale and lose my appetite. My stepmother told papa I was fretted. He called me to him and asked me to talk it out, papa did. 'It's simple,' I said, 'I don't want to go.'

'It's goin' to be all right, Sinney, me and ma will go with you a bit.'

'But you won't stay,' I went on. 'You'll leave me and come back here, and I'll be shut up with a woman that's goin' to teach me. I can't do it!'

'It seems to me like, Sinney, you ain't in love with Joe.'

'Yes, I love him, I love him plenty if he'd stay here. I want to be his wife—if I can live like other women and go to housekeepin' like my sisters.'

Papa said: 'You're goin' into a great deal higher company than your sisters ever traveled in. You're goin' to be made a lady of, a Southern lady. I know their class and they is sweet women.'

I went home with papa; and when Joe come back to Nancy's he borrowed a horse and rode over. It was near winter. We had a big fire going. First supper. We set round after; then me and Joe walked out through the trees. If I go to Kentucky with Joe, I thought, I'll never see them old leaves fallin' again.

But there wasn't a word said about it then. When it come bedtime, me and him went outdoors to let the family turn in. They was sound asleep when we come back and set down by the fire. Sure, when I had a beau, I had to do my sparking in front of the old folks. It was all done in the same room. They turned their backs.

Well, I up and told Joe. He tried everything but I stuck to my point. Joe had to go back to Nancy's; he was finishing up his business around there. Nancy took a hand in it, too. She told me how much better I'd be off than her and the rest of the girls. 'You are missin' the best thing that you'll ever come up against in your life. You'll never have to work none.'

'I ain't afraid of work!'

But Nancy didn't feel that way about it. 'I'd marry him; I'd marry him quick!' she said.

It ended up just as I say. Joe had to go home but he'd be back in three months. He come back; I should say he did. I was over to Susan's meanwhile. And inside that time I got to going with Williamson Page and getting very much interested in him. Willie was about twenty-nine years old and a plain kind of country boy, one of my own class. A farm boy.

SCHOOL OF EDUCATION
CURRICULUM LABORATORY
UM-DEARBORN

My brother Alfred took me to my father's. Joe was waiting for me; we set and hashed it all out but it wasn't no use. He loved me, Joe did; he knew I was an innocent girl and he'd seen a lot of the other kind in his twenty-four years, like them city boys does. Joe was always giving advice. 'Don't ever let no man lollygag you,' he used to say.

Joe was leaving and he looked pretty blue. Going back he'd have to travel by the graveyard where Hennie Fuel was buried. 'Joe,' I said, 'stop and look over the wall and think to yourself, would you rather be layin' there like him, or turned loose, with a blessin' for your happiness?'

'I can tell you now,' he said, 'I'd rather be as I am. . . . But I care a lot, and I'd have liked to have proved it to you.' He turned around and took me in his arms and hugged me.

'Remember what I told you about other men,' he said. Joe wasn't thinking about himself, he was like that.

I mightn't have married Willie Page if it hadn't been for all I heard around there about the Page name. Specially old man Page. He was very wealthy and give them all a home—every one of his ten children—eighty acres of land each, there in Hendricks County.

I'd be hearing, too, what Willie Page said, when I was only a child, that he was 'goin' to wait till that little red-head sister of Alfred's grows up.' He said it the day brother Alfred married Rebecca McCloud. Rebecca's mother was Willie Page's sister.

Willie waited on me for a year even after I was growed up. Alfred told him to take it cool. 'She's red-headed, you can't drive her, but she'll come round!' Alfred was strong for Willie. . . . But my stepmother's nephew, Harry Staton, come mighty close to busting in on Willie. 'Uncle' Joe Staton was the richest man in them parts and Harry was his only child.

One of the neighbor girls was out in our yard seeing if I'd go to church with her next day, over to Haw Creek. I was in the shade washing my go-to-meeting dress. We had a cow in the clover patch, right close by the house, and next to it was a cornfield but no fence between. Papa was setting on the porch and he sung out, 'Sinney, the cow's in the corn, run her out!' I started off flying but I stepped in a hole and fell down.

'Goddamn that old post-hole, anyway!' Hearing me say that, not over twenty foot off, was two young men dismounting by the gate! And there I was, a young girl, swearing and cussing. Sure, I felt ashamed.

They was going into the house, but I cut across the clover patch, up to sister Betty's as fast as I could travel.

Betty told me, 'It serves you right, Linney, a-cussin'.'

'Aw,' I said, 'it jes' slipped out.'

I waited at Betty's quite a while and kept watching. Them horses still stood there. Then somebody come out and started leading them over to the barn.

'You're in for it now,' Betty said, 'it must be some kin of mother's and they're stayin' for the night. Streak for home and get on some nice clothes. Jes' walk down bold-like and be introduced.'

I done it and it worked fine. This young fellow, Harry Staton, asked me could he go with me next day to church. Sunday evening he asked me could he come back in a week. I told him no, he could come the Sunday after that. Willie Page had been coming to see me every second Sunday and this happened to be Willie's off Sunday. No, I didn't want no tangle.

It went on for five months like that and I was kind of up against it. Willie Page or Harry Staton? I couldn't decide which. Willie was always rubbing up against me and filching kisses, but the other one—never.

I told my stepmother I didn't know which I liked best.

'In accordance with that I don't believe you're much in love with either of them.'

And truthfully I don't believe I was myself, when I come to find out what love is.

Willie asked me to marry him but I wouldn't give him no decision. And the next week I said something to Harry that hurt his feelings—I accused him of going with some other girl—and land sakes, if he didn't propose to me!

I believe now it would have been best if I had married Harry. Harry was a goer; he was a money-maker and out of a fine family. Not that Willie wasn't of good stock too, but he was the baby and spoilt. He hadn't been made to work; he didn't know what it was like. . . .

In about a month, I guess it was, I told Willie Page I'd marry him. It was right after the end of the Civil War. Papa had just bought my sister Susan's place and give Alfred the old homestead. We was married at Alfred's, on a Sunday forenoon, by old Adam Feathers. Then he goes over to the church after he marries us and tells the congregation about it. 'I'm come from joinin' Abe Plunkett's Linney,' he said, 'and Williamson Page!'

After meeting they all come over to papa's house where the wedding cake was baked and everything set for a big dinner. Me and Willie wasn't there. We lit out. We knew they'd be fixing for a shivaree and we dodged them. Jumped our horses and went to my husband's sister's place for the night. We was hiding out. We was ten miles from the old homestead.

Next day when we got back my sister Betty come up to me. 'I got something to tell you,' she said. 'Everybody was happy, and wishin' you much joy, and eatin' the cake, but one.'

'Who was that?'

'Sammy Booker!'

Sammy had been trying to go with me, and papa and his father had talked it all over and wanted us to get hitched. They promised each to give us forty acres of their land that joined. Eighty acres, quite a temptation for two young 'uns. But I didn't take to Sammy. He was a fine boy but he had ground-hog teeth. His upper lip wouldn't cover them. I never seen so many teeth put together in one mouth!

One time papa asked me, 'What have you got against Sammy? Is there somebody you like better?'

I answered him, 'Don't you think a woman wants to be kissed by her husband? How the devil's Sammy goin' to do it?' Wasn't that an awful thing to throw up against anybody? God a'mighty's truth, I did think of that! . . .

We had been away from Boone County two dry years; two years of terrible crops. As lean as they was in the Wabash Valley we fared better than our Boone County tenent. He hadn't nothing to show for his toil and owed us two years' rent. He done the only thing the poor man could. 'Page,' he said to Willie, 'move in now 'stead of next March and take the crop for what it's worth. It's the only way I can pay you at all.'

It felt good to be back home and I thought maybe everything was going to go all right—even though we didn't have a dollar, only from what we gathered up and sold on the Burroughs place.

In March, following that fall, I fell sick with pneumonia. We'd been doing middling good, what I called blundering through. I know how I caught it—going out milking the cow in the cold. I didn't take care of myself—never had no time, the way Willie dawdled and loafed and left things undone.

The doctor's name was Tinkler, watching over me through this spell. I had five blisters that et into my flesh until there was sores like holes. We didn't have no cabbage like he ordered, but Annie Shepard, my sister-in-law, bless her, had it growing and she come and showed them how to manage it, drawing the corruption out with wilted, green cabbage leaves.

I couldn't stand a man that would let me suffer while he toasted his feet in front of the fire. I suffered terrible. I'd be crying, and asking Willie to put on some fresh cabbage. 'I will,' he'd say, 'jes' so soon as I finish my pipe.' Put-offs like that.

The God I believe in today is the power that's in us to do good. But them days I believed like the rest of them. I prayed to God to please to let me get out of that bed. I lay there crazy with worry. I seen how it was. I thought: Everything that he's ever had in life was give him. He ain't the sort to go to the bottom and climb up. It's up to yourself, or the Lord help you and your little ones!

I kept thinking what Willie should have done and hadn't. I had the time to study it out. I made up my mind it was sink or swim, and saddled to Willie we'd all sink. Leave him! Staying there meant hardship and want for the rest of my life. I was praying for the chance to find something else for my children. I promised God I would, if only I'd get well.

I cured up awful slow. On Ollie's birthday, the twenty-fifth of May—I couldn't much more than drag myself around the house—I made the children as nice a birthday party as I was able. I knowed it was the last meal of vittles I'd be fixing them.

Mind you, I never had been away from them a day. I washed their little feet and cleaned them up like always, before I put them to bed and kissed them goodnight. Next morning I said as how I was going to see their Aunt Mary down in Texas. Then I was coming back to fetch them. . . .

Ollie was standing, leaning up against the mantel piece. May asked him, 'What are you doin', are you cryin'?' She was about five years old, she couldn't understand.

'Well, don't YOU feel bad,' he said; 'don't you know that mama's a-leavin' us and a-goin' away? Ain't I got plenty to make me feel bad?' Ollie was nine.

'She'll come back after us,' May said, 'she told me so, and Aunt Sally's a-goin' to care for us meantime.'

TWO YEARS MALINDA WAS MANAGING A BOARDING HOUSE IN HOT SPRINGS, ARKANSAS. SHE HAD OBTAINED A DIVORCE AND TAKEN HER CHILDREN TO LIVE WITH RELATIVES IN TEXAS.

You know there's such a thing as Fate. Deny it all you want, but it's there just the same. Everybody that's had anything happen to them knows what I mean. I had been running the Mountain House a month or so when Jim, the stage-driver, told Ida that he had picked up a fine-looking, well-dressed man at the station. Just off the train. This man wanted a good place to board.

Jim said, 'I been taking some people over yonder to the Mountain House and they seem well content. It belongs to a young widow from Texas.'

It was Jenkins. He answered Jim back, 'Take me to the widow from Texas; she's my meat!'

But I didn't find that out for a week. The night that Jim was telling about, the clerk come to my room to say as there was two men downstairs asking for a front room.

'Tell 'em to wait,' I said. I put on a black velvet dress that had a red silk, pleated ruffle under the skirt. Then I put on a gold colored polonaise and took a good look in the glass before I went down.

A strange feeling come over me when I seen him. I could have painted his picture; but the other man setting beside him, I'll never know what he looked like. Something said to me, 'You have met your fate but fight it!'

Jenky was there three days when he paid me a month's bill in advance. I couldn't figure that out, what he aimed to do at Hot Springs for a month.

The next night he tried hard to get thick, and after a time he asked me to go to the park with him. But I couldn't stop for no nonsense. Then come up that thing that Ida was telling me and it riled me so bad I wouldn't speak to him—I passed him in the hall without even saying howdy.

Behaving like that made me blue though; I was acting against my feelings. I wasn't happy. Could it be that I had fallen for this youngster? I couldn't make it out at all—still I wouldn't give in.

Then Jenky made believe he was sick, and in the morning someone wanted to know would I look after him until the doctor come. I said as he was living in my place I'd have to do anything I could for him. I went up to Jenky's room and he asked me to put cold towels on his head. Pretty soon he confessed he wasn't sick at all and before I could tell him all the cutting things that come into my head, before I could get a word out, he'd proposed to me.

'I can't stand your bein' so near me and not havin' you. . . . Seein' how you won't take me no other way, maybe you'll marry me?'

'No!' I said, and I rushed out of the room.

He asked me three times more, once across the office desk! He said he knew I had a little girl and he'd care for her as if she was his own.

'No, I ain't goin' to marry you, I don't want to have nothin' to do with you.'

'Well then, I ain't stayin' on where I can see you, I'm a-goin' over to Texarkana.' And that was the smartest thing Jenky ever done in his life.

Before he left he asked me would I call for his watch where he left it to be fixed, and hold it until he let me know where to send it. I said I would if there wasn't no other way.

I was trying to fight my fate and it got me into bed. I lay there three days thinking my head would split open. Then the feeling come over me that I must get out of town and run away from everything that reminded me of Jenky.

I settled my affairs and bought me a ticket to Fort Worth. I sent Jenky a telegram to Texarkana to meet me at the station when the train went through and I would give him his watch. Back come a telegram from him saying, 'Buy a ticket to Texarkana instead of Fort Worth.'

But my mind was made up and I didn't do it. I traveled all that night. The next day, about fifty miles outside of Texarkana, Jenky boarded the train. He come in the car and set down and my heart sunk inside me.

'I'm goin' to ask a favor of you,' he begun. 'It won't put you out none. I want you to stay over until eight o'clock tonight and take the late train to Fort Worth. I have engaged a nice room for you where you can rest and clean up and my landlady is goin' to cook your dinner.'

Well, I thought, I can gratify him that far. So I said all right, I would.

He must have told the woman where he boarded about me for she praised him up to the skies, what a fine fellow he was. And Jenky talked and talked until it was six o'clock in the evening. 'It's all up to you,' he said. 'I've told you everything there's to tell. You know I am a gambler; I ain't got a dollar in my pocket this minute. But that don't signify nothin'; I'll have money again.' He was a loser then; but he was a money-maker, too. He never stopped, he never quit, he knew that he would make it some time. . . .

Something said to me, Why don't you risk it? Against that I kept saying to myself: Fight it! Fight it!

One thing I couldn't deny. I was in love with him; it was all I could do to keep from throwing myself in his arms.

Suddenly it come to me: Try it even if it only lasts a year, and the worst that can happen, if it comes to the worst, you can divorce him. Divorcing was more than a sneeze them days. I was scared at myself for thinking of it, but I was crazy for the man and there wasn't nothing I didn't think of, trying not to give him up.

Jenky was a handsome scamp but I often thought about it since —maybe I was more in love with love than with the man. God knows, I'd gone all my life without it. And all the other things I thought of, along with love. A fine home and children around me, no end of children. That was the picture that was framed in my heart. I was obliged to change the frame but the picture was always there. It still is. I long for the same things today as when I was Willie Page's bride. But now my life's behind me.

I learned more from Jenky than all the others put together. I oughtn't have married him but he was the man I wanted and I had to. I was horrified at his gambling. I had the big head; I thought I was better than some people. But I couldn't get away from Jenky, he was too slick. His way of making love was different. There was no lovey-dovey. He was artful; he dug hisself into my heart.

Even after I promised Jenky to marry him it was hard for me to go through with it. I was that narrow, if I'd seen a fast woman coming towards me I'd have crossed the street, afeared of tainture. And gamblers belonged to the same breed.

Jenky loved me as much as a gambler could love anything outside of four aces. Down deep though I wouldn't call it love; he wanted me, and I expect he admired me. And out of it all come the suffering and the laughter. . . .

I knowed what I was doing; my eyes was wide open and I bunched into it. I wanted one year of love that I'd been afire for—even if it meant fifty years of hell. Well now, I done better than that.

When Jenky walked off from the Mountain House at Hot Springs he left behind a month's rent that was due him. I couldn't make him take it. But when he goes to marry me a few days later, in Texarkana, at the office of the Justice of the Peace, my money bought the marriage license. 'I'm short of money, dear,' was what he said.

Back that time at the Mountain House, when Jenky paid his month in advance, I had my purse in my bosom. The stairway come down into a kind of social hall, and I walked over to the stairs with my back to him and counted out the change. Years after, you see, when some people was talking to Jenky about love and such like, and they asked him, 'How come you, a young man, to marry a woman with three children?' here's the answer he give them, just to show you how cute he was. 'Hell,' he said, 'what did I care? When I went to pay her the room rent she set her foot on the stairway and under the red ruffles, round the bottom of her skirt, I seen her leg. Nothin' could have stopped me askin' her!

He never told me for all them years, until he sputtered it out in front of a lot of people.

We was married June 14, 1883. At seven o'clock at night in Texarkana. Eight o'clock next morning we went on to Fort Worth. Jenky was a stranger there and his idea was to go West but I wanted to go home to May.

The first thing I done wrong, I asked Jenky for his overcoat that was rolled up in the train rack; I was cold. I spread it over me to keep me warm and when we got off the train we was in such a rush I forgot it. A beautiful black overcoat, too. He never got it back; it just made me have to buy him a new one.

We stayed in Fort Worth three or four weeks. We went and got May and took her out riding. She didn't like it, she kept looking at Jenky and sizing him up.

'Listen here,' I whispered to her on the side, 'don't you like your new papa?'

'How many papas am I goin' to have?'

Mormon Polygamy

The polygamous marriages practiced by the Mormon pioneers of Utah were unique in the history of the American frontier. In the following letter a Mormon wife tries to explain polygamy to her sister in New England. What arguments did she use? Are they persuasive? Do you think her sister would be convinced? Do you think the writer of the letter was convinced? What disadvantages might polygamy have that she hasn't considered? (Richard F. Burton, The City of the Saints *(1857), 484-93.)*

Great Salt Lake City, Jan. 12, 1854.

DEAR SISTER, —Your letter of Oct. 2 was received on yesterday. My joy on its reception was more than I can express. I had waited so long for your answer to our last, that I had almost concluded my friends were offended, and would write to me no more. Judge, then, of my joy when I read the sentiments of friendship and of sisterly affection expressed in your letter.

We are all well here, and are prosperous and happy in our family circle. My children, four in number, are healthy and cheerful, and fast expanding their physical and intellectual faculties. Health, peace, and prosperity have attended us all the day long.

It seems, my dear sister, that we are no nearer together in our religious views than formerly. Why is this? Are we not all bound to leave this world, with all we possess therein, and reap the reward of our doings *here* in a never-ending hereafter? If so, do we not desire to be undeceived, and to *know and to do the truth?* Do we not all wish in our very hearts to be sincere with ourselves, and to be honest and frank with each other?

If so, you will bear with me patiently, while I give a few of my reasons for embracing, and holding sacred, that particular point in the doctrine of the Church of the Saints to which you, my dear sister, together with a large majority of Christendom, so decidedly object. I mean, a *"plurality of wives."*

I have a Bible, which I have been taught from my infancy to hold sacred. In this Bible, I read of a holy man named Abraham, who is represented as the friend of God, a faithful man in all things, a man who kept the commandments of God, and who is called, in the New Testament, "the father of the faithful." See James ii. 23; Rom. iv. 16; Gal. iii. 8, 9, 16, 29.

I find this man had a plurality of wives, some of which were called concubines. See Book of Genesis; and for his concubines, see xxv. 6.

I also find his grandson Jacob possessed of four wives, twelve sons, and a daughter. These wives are spoken very highly of, by the sacred writers as honourable and virtuous women. *"These,"* say the Scriptures, *"did build the house of Israel."*

Jacob himself was also a man of God, and the Lord blessed him and his house, and commanded him to be fruitful and multiply. See Gen. xxx. to xxxv. and particularly xxxv. 10, 11.

I find also that the twelve sons of Jacob, by these four wives, became princes, heads of tribes, patriarchs, whose names are had in everlasting remembrance to all generations.

Now God talked with Abraham, Isaac, and Jacob frequently; and His angels also visited and talked with them, and blessed them and their wives and children. He also reproved the sins of some of the sons of Jacob, for hating and selling their brother, and for adultery. But in all His communications with them, He never condemned their family organisation; but, on the contrary, always approved of it, and blessed them in this respect. He even told Abraham that He would make him the father of many nations, and that in him and his seed all the nations and kindreds of the earth should be blessed. See Genesis xviii. 17-19; also xii. 1-3. In later years I find the plurality of wives perpetuated, sanctioned, and provided for in the law of Moses.

David the Psalmist not only had a plurality of wives, but the Lord

Himself spoke by the mouth of Nathan the Prophet, and told David that *He* (the Lord) had given his master's wives into his bosom; but because he had committed adultery with the wife of Uriah, and had caused his murder, *He* would take *his* wives and give them to a neighbour of his, &c. See 2 Samuel xii. 7-11.

Here, then, we have the word of the Lord, not only sanctioning polygamy, but actually giving to king David the wives of his master (Saul), and afterward taking the wives of David from him, and giving them to another man. Here we have a sample of severe reproof and punishment for adultery and murder, while polygamy is authorised and approved by the word of God.

But to come to the New Testament. I find Jesus Christ speaks very highly of Abraham and his family. He says, *"Many shall come from the east, and from the west, and from the north, and from the south, and shall sit down with Abraham, Isaac, and Jacob, in the kingdom of God."* Luke xiii. 28, 29.

Again he said, *"If ye were Abraham's seed, ye would do the works of Abraham."*

Paul the Apostle wrote to the saints of his day, and informed them as follows: "As many of you as have been baptized into Christ have put on Christ; and if ye are Christ's, then are ye Abraham's seed, and heirs according to the promise."

He also sets forth Abraham and Sarah as patterns of faith and good works, and as the father and mother of faithful Christians, who should, by faith and good works, aspire to be counted the sons of Abraham and daughters of Sarah.

Now let us look at some of the works of Sarah, for which she is so highly commended by the Apostles, and by them held up as a pattern for Christian ladies to imitate. *"Now Sarah, Abram's wife, bare him no children; and she had a handmaid, an Egyptian, whose name was Hagar. And Sarah said unto Abram, Behold now, the Lord hath restrained me from bearing: I pray thee go in unto my maid: it may be that I may obtain children of her. And Abram hearkened unto the voice of Sarah. And Sarah, Abram's wife, took Hagar her maid, the Egyptian, after Abram had dwelt ten years in the land of Canaan, and gave her to her husband, Abram, to be his wife."* See Genesis xvi. 1-3.

According to Jesus Christ and the Apostles, then, the only way to be saved is to be adopted into the great family of polygamists, by the Gospel, and then strictly follow their examples.

Again, John the Revelator describes the Holy City of the heavenly Jerusalem, with the names of the twelve sons of Jacob inscribed on the gates. Rev. xxi 12.

To sum up the whole, then, I find that polygamists were the friends of God; that the family and lineage of a polygamist were selected, in which all nations should be blessed; that a polygamist is named in the New Testament as the father of the faithful Christians of after ages, and cited as a pattern for all generations; that the wife of a polygamist, who encouraged her husband in the practice of the same, and even urged him into it, and officiated in giving him another wife, is named as an honourable and virtuous woman, a pattern for Christian ladies, and the very mother of all holy women in the Christian Church, whose aspiration it should be to be called her daughters; that Jesus Christ has declared that the great fathers of the polygamic family stand at the head in the kingdom of good; in short, that all the saved of after generations should be saved by becoming members of a polygamic family; that all those who do not become members of it are strangers and aliens to the covenant of promise, the commonwealth of Israel, and not heirs according to the promise made to Abraham; that all people from the east, west, north, or south, who enter into the kingdom, enter into the society of polygamists, and under their patriarchal rule and government; indeed, no one can even approach the gates of heaven without beholding the names of twelve polygamists (the sons of four different women by one man) engraven in everlasting glory upon the pearly gates.

My dear sister, with the Scriptures before me, I could never find it in my heart to reject the heavenly vision which has restored to man the fulness of the Gospel, or the Latter Day Prophets and Apostles, merely because in this restoration is included the ancient law of matrimony and of family organisation and government, preparatory to the restoration of all Israel.

But, leaving all Scripture, history, or precedent out of the question, let us come to nature's law. What, then, appears to be the great object of the marriage relations? I answer, the multiplying of our species, the rearing and training of children.

To accomplish this object, natural law would dictate that a husband should remain apart from his wife at certain seasons, which, in the very constitution of the female, are untimely; or, in other words, indulgence should be not merely for pleasure or wanton desires, but mainly for the purpose of procreation.

The mortality of nature would teach a mother, that, during nature's process in the formation and growth of embryo man, her heart should be pure, her thoughts and affections chaste, her mind calm, her passions without excitement, while her body should be invigorated with every exercise conducive to health and vigour, but by no means subjected to anything calculated to disturb, irritate, weary, or exhaust any of its functions.

And while a kind husband should nourish, sustain, and comfort the wife of his bosom by every kindness and attention consistent with her situation, and with his most tender affection; still he should refrain from all those untimely associations which are forbidden in the great constitutional laws of female nature; which laws we see carried out in almost the entire animal economy, human animals excepted.

Polygamy, then, as practised under the Patriarchal law of God, tends directly to the chastity of women, and to sound health and morals in the constitutions of their offspring.

You can read, in the law of God, in your Bible, the times and circumstances under which a woman should remain apart from her husband, during which times she is considered unclean; and should her husband come to her bed under such circumstances, he would commit a gross sin both against the laws of nature and the wise provisions of God's law, as revealed in His word; in short, he would commit an abomination; he would sin both against his own body, against the body of his wife, and against the laws of procreation, in which the health and morals of his offspring are directly concerned.

The polygamic law of God opens to all vigorous, healthy, and virtuous females a door by which they may become honourable wives of virtuous men, and mothers of faithful, virtuous, healthy, and vigorous children.

And here let me ask you, my dear sister, what female in all New Hampshire would marry a drunkard, a man of hereditary disease, a debauchee, an idler, or a spendthrift; or what woman would become a prostitute, or, on the other hand, live and die single, or without forming those inexpressibly dear relationships of wife and mother, if the Abrahamic covenant, or Patriarchal laws of God, were extended over your State, and held sacred and honourable by all?

Dear sister, in your thoughtlessness, you inquire, "Why not a plurality of husbands as well as a plurality of wives?" To which I reply: 1st, God has never commanded or sanctioned a plurality of husbands; 2nd, *"Man is the head of the woman,"* and no woman can serve two lords; 3rd, Such an order of things would work death and not life, or, in plain language, it would multiply disease instead of children. In fact, the experiment of a plurality of husbands, or rather of one woman for many men, is in active operation, and has been, for centuries, in all the principal towns and cities of *"Christendom!"* It is the genius of *"Christian instututions,"* falsely so called. It is the result of *"Mystery Babylon, the great whore of all the earth."* Or in other words, it is the result of making void the holy ordinances of God in relation to matrimony, and introducing the laws of Rome, in which the clergy and nuns are forbidden to marry, and other members only permitted to have one wife. This law leaves females exposed to a life of single *"blessedness,"* without husband, child, or friend to provide for or comfort them; or to a life of poverty and loneliness, exposed to temptation, to perverted affections, to unlawful means to gratify them, or to the necessity of selling themselves for lucre. While the man who has abundance of means is tempted to spend it on a mistress in secret, and in a lawless way, the law of God would have given her to him as an honourable wife. These circumstances give rise to murder, infanticide, suicide, disease, remorse, despair, wretchedness, poverty, untimely death, with all the attendant train of jealousies, heartrending miseries, want of confidence in families, contaminating disease, &c.; and finally, to the horrible license system, in which governments, called Christian, license their fair daughters, I will not say to play the beast, but to a degradation far beneath them; for every species of the animal creation, except man, refrain from such abominable excesses, and observe in a great measure the laws of nature in procreation.

I again repeat, that nature has constituted the female differently from the male; and for a different purpose. The strength of the female constitution is designed to flow in a stream of *life*, to nourish and sustain the embryo, to bring it forth, and to nurse it on her bosom. When nature is not in operation within her in these particulars, and for these heavenly ends, it has wisely provided relief at regular periods, in order that her system may be kept pure and healthy, without exhausting the fountain of life on the one hand, or drying up its river of life on the other; till mature age, and an approaching change of worlds, render it necessary for her to cease to be fruitful, and give her to rest awhile, and enjoy a tranquil life in the midst of that family circle, endeared to her by so many ties, and which may be supposed, at this period of her life, to be approaching the vigour of manhood, and therefore able to comfort and sustain her.

Not so with man. He has no such drawback upon his strength. It is his to move in a wider sphere. If God shall count him worthy of an hundred fold, in this life, of wives and children, and houses, and lands, and kindreds, he may even aspire to Patriarchal sovereignty, to empire; to be the prince or head of a tribe, or tribes; and like Abraham of old, be able to send forth, for the defence of his country, hundreds and thousands of his own warriors, born in his own house.

A noble man of God, who is full of the Spirit of the Most High, and is counted worthy to converse with Jehovah, or with the Son of God; and to associate with angels, and the spirits of just men made perfect; one who will teach his children, and bring them up in the light of unadulterated and eternal truth; is more worthy of a hundred wives and children, than the ignorant slave of passion, or of vice and folly, is to have one wife and one child. Indeed the God of Abraham is so much better pleased with one than with the other, that he would even take away the one talent, which is habitually abused, neglected, or put to an improper use, and give it to him who has ten talents.

In the Patriarchal order of family government, the wife is bound to the law of her husband. She honours, *"calls him lord,"* even as Sarah obeyed and honoured Abraham. She lives for him, and to increase his glory, his greatness, his kingdom, or family. Her affections are centred in her God, her husband, and her children.

The children are also under his government, worlds without end. *"While life or thought, or being lasts, or immortality endures,"* they are bound to obey him as their father and king.

He also has a head, to whom he is responsible. He must keep the commandments of God, and observe His laws. He must not take a wife unless she is given to him by the law and authority of God. He must not commit adultery, nor take liberties with any woman except his own, who are secured to him by the holy ordinances of matrimony.

Hence a nation organised under the law of the Gospel, or in other words, the law of Abraham and the Patriarchs, would have no institutions tending to licentiousness; no adulteries, fornications, &c., would be tolerated. No houses or institutions would exist for traffic in shame, or in the life-blood of our fair daughters. Wealthy men would have no inducement to keep a mistress in secret, or unlawfully. Females would have no grounds for temptation in any such lawless life. Neither money nor pleasure could tempt them, nor poverty drive them to any such excess; because the door would be open for every virtuous female to form the honourable and endearing relationships of wife and mother, in some virtuous family, where love, and peace, and plenty would crown her days, and truth and the practice of virtue qualify her to be transplanted with her family circle in that eternal soil, where they might multiply their children, without pain, or sorrow, or death; and go on increasing in numbers, in wealth, in greatness, in glory, might, majesty, power, and dominion, in worlds without end.

O my dear sister! could the dark veil of tradition be rent from your mind! could you gaze for a moment on the resurrection of the just! could you behold Abraham, Isaac, and Jacob, and their wives and children, clad in the bloom, freshness, and beauty of immortal *flesh and bones;* clothed in robes of fine white linen, bedecked with precious stones and gold; and surrounded with an offspring of immortals as countless as the stars of the firmament, or as the grains of sand upon the sea shore; over which they reign as kings and queens for ever and ever! you would then know something of the weight of those words of the sacred writer which are recorded in relation to the four wives of Jacob, the mothers of the twelve Patriarchs, namely: *"These did build the house of Israel."*

O that my dear kindred could but realise that they have need to repent of the sins, ignorance, and traditions of those perverted systems which are misnamed *"Christianity,"* and be baptized—*buried* in the water, in the likeness of the death and burial of Jesus Christ, and rise to newness of life in the likeness of his resurrection; receive his Spirit by the laying on of the hands of an Apostle, according to promise, and forsake the world and the pride thereof. Thus they would be adopted into the family of Abraham, become his sons and daughters, see and enjoy for themselves the visions of the Spirit of eternal truth, which bear witness of the family order of heaven, and the beauties and glories of eternal kindred ties; for my pen can never describe them.

Dear, *dear* kindred: remember, according to the New Testament, and the testimony of an ancient Apostle, if you are ever saved in the kingdom of God, it must be by being adopted into the family of polygamists—the family of the great Patriarch Abraham: for in his seed, or family, and not out of it, *"shall all the nations and kindreds of the earth be blessed."*

You say you believe polygamy is *"licentiousness;"* that it is *"abominable,"* *"beastly,"* &c.; "the practice only of the most barbarous nations, or of the dark ages, or of some great or good men who were left to commit gross sins." Yet you say you are anxious for me to be converted to your faith; and that we may see each other in this life, and be associated in one great family in that life which has no end.

Now in order to comply with your wishes, I must renounce the Old and New Testaments; must count Abraham, Isaac, and Jacob, and their families, as licentious, wicked, beastly, abominable characters; Moses, Nathan, David, and the Prophets, no better. I must look upon the God of Israel as partaker in all these abominations, by holding them in fellowship; and even as a minister of such iniquity, by giving king Saul's wives into king David's bosom; and afterwards by taking David's wives from him, and giving them to his neighbour. I must consider Jesus Christ, and Paul, and John, as either living in a dark age, as full of the darkness and ignorance of barbarous climes, or else wilfully abominable and wicked, in fellowshipping polygamists, and representing them as fathers of the faithful, and rulers in heaven. I must doom them all to hell, with adulterers, fornicators, &c., or else, at least, assign to them some nook or corner in heaven, as ignorant persons, who, knowing but little, were beaten with few stripes. While, by analogy, I must learn to consider the Roman Popes, clergy, and nuns, who do not marry at all, as foremost in the ranks of glory; and those Catholics and Protestants who have but one wife, as next in order of salvation, glory, immortality, and eternal life.

Now, dear friends, much as I long to see you, and dear as you are to me, I can never come to these terms. I feel as though the Gospel had introduced me into the right family, into the right lineage, and into good company. And besides all these considerations, should I ever become so beclouded with unbelief of the Scriptures and heavenly institutions, as to agree with my kindred in New Hampshire, in *theory*, still my practical circumstances are different, and would I fear continue to separate us by a wide and almost impassable gulf.

For instance, I have (as you see, in all good conscience, founded on the word of God) formed family and kindred ties, which are inexpressibly dear to me, and which I can never bring my feelings to consent to dissolve. I have a good and virtuous husband whom I love. We have four little children which are mutually and inexpressibly dear to us. And besides this my husband has seven other living wives, and one who has departed to a better world. He has in all upwards of twenty-five children. All these mothers and children are endeared to me by kindred ties, by mutual affection, by acquaintance and association; and the mothers in particular, by mutual and long-continued exercises of toil, patience, long-suffering, and sisterly kindness. We all have our imperfections in this life; but I know that these are good and worthy women, and that my husband is a good and worthy man; one who keeps the commandments of Jesus Christ, and presides in his family like an Abraham. He seeks to provide for them with all diligence; he loves them all, and seeks to comfort them and make them happy. He teaches them the commandments of Jesus Christ, and gathers them about him in the family circle to call upon his God, both morning and evening. He and his family have the confidence, esteem, good-will, and fellowship of this entire territory, and of a wide circle of acquaintances in Europe and America. He is a practical teacher of morals and religion, a promoter of general education, and at present occupies an honourable seat in the Legislative Council of this territory.

Now, as to visiting my kindred in New Hampshire, I would be pleased to do so, were it the will of God. But first, the laws of that state must be so modified by enlightened legislation, and the customs and consciences of its inhabitants, and of my kindred, so altered, that my husband can accompany me with all his wives and children, and be as much respected and honoured in his family organisation, and in his holy calling, as he is at home; or in the same manner as the Patriarch Jacob would have been respected, had he, with his wives and children, paid a visit to his kindred. As my husband is yet in his youth, as well as myself, I fondly hope we shall live to see that day. For already the star of Jacob is in the ascendency; the house of Israel is about to be restored: while *"Mystery Babylon,"* with all her institutions, awaits her own overthrow. Till this is the case in New Hampshire, my kindred will be under the necessity of coming here to see us, or, on the other hand, we will be mutually compelled to forego the pleasure of each other's company.

You mention, in your letter, that Paul, the Apostle, recommended that Bishops be the husband of one wife. Why this was the case, I do not know, unless it was, as he says, that while he was among Romans he did as Romans did. Rome, at that time, governed the world, as it were; and although gross idolaters, they held to the one wife system. Under these circumstances, no doubt, the Apostle Paul, seeing a great many polygamists in the Church, recommended that they had better choose for this particular temporal office, men of small families, who would not be in disrepute with the government. This is precisely our course in those countries where Roman institutions still bear sway. Our Elders there have but one wife, in order to conform to the laws of men.

You inquire why Elder W., when at your house, denied that the Church of this age held to the doctrine of plurality. I answer, that he might have been ignorant of the fact, as our belief on this point was not published till 1852. And had he known it, he had no right to reveal the same until the full time had arrived. God kindly withheld this doctrine for a time, because of the ignorance and prejudice of the nations of mystic Babylon, that peradventure he might save some of them.

Now, dear sister, I must close. I wish all my kindred and old acquaintances to see this letter, or a copy thereof; and that they will consider it as if written to themselves. I love them dearly, and greatly desire and pray for their salvation, and that we may all meet with Abraham, Isaac, and Jacob, in the kingdom of God.

Dear sister, do not let your prejudices and traditions keep you from believing the Bible; nor the pride, shame, or love of the world keep you from your seat in the kingdom of heaven, among the royal family of polygamists. Write often and freely.

With sentiments of the deepest affection and kindred feeling, I remain, dear sister, your affectionate sister,

BELINDA MARDEN PRATT.

IV. WORK AND PLAY

A great many Americans have always believed that the frontier West was a place of great opportunity, sudden riches, and romantic adventure. Do the following passages support this belief? How different were the working conditions of men and women? How similar? What satisfactions were there to be had? What displeasures? What sustained people in their lives on the frontier?

Being a Cowboy

The boyhood ambition of Charles Siringo, as we have seen, was to be a cowboy. Were his actual experiences what he expected? How would you describe the life he led? What were the rewards of that kind of life? What were the difficulties? Did he like the way he lived? (Siringo, A Texas Cowboy, *83-93)*

We arrived in Kiowa, a little one-horse town on the Medicine, about dark one cold and disagreeable evening.

We put up at the Davis House, which was kept by a man named Davis—by the way one of the whitest men that ever wore shoes. Collier made arrangements that night with Mr. Davis to board us on "tick" until we could get work. But I wouldn't agree to that.

The next morning after paying my night's lodging I had just one dollar left and I gave that to Mr. Collier as I bade him adieu. I then headed southwest across the hills, not having any destination in view; I wanted to go somewhere but didn't care where. To tell the truth I was still somewhat rattled over my recent bad luck.

That night I lay out in the brush by myself and next morning changed my course to southeast, down a creek called Driftwood. About noon I accidentally landed in Gus Johnson's Cow camp at the forks of Driftwood and "Little Mule" creeks.

I remained there all night and next morning when I was fixing to pull out—God only knows where, the boss, Bill Hudson, asked me if I wouldn't stay and work in his place until he went to Hutchison, Kansas and back? I agreed to do so finally if he would furnish "Whiskey-peat," my pony, all the corn he could eat—over and above my wages, which were to be twenty-five dollars a month. The outfit consisted of only about twenty-five hundred Texas steers, a chuck wagon, cook and five riders besides the boss.

A few days after Mr. Hudson left we experienced a terrible severe snow storm. We had to stay with the drifting herd night and day, therefore it went rough with us—myself especially, being from a warm climate and only clad in common garments, while the other boys were fixed for winter.

When Mr. Hudson came back from Hutchison he pulled up stakes and drifted south down into the Indian territory—our camp was then on the territory and Kansas line—in search of good winter quarters.

We located on the "Eagle Chief" river, a place where cattle had never been held before. Cattlemen in that section of country considered it better policy to hug the Kansas line on account of indians.

About the time we became settled in our new quarters, my month was up and Mr. Hudson paid me twenty-five dollars, telling me to make that my home all winter if I wished.

My "pile" now amounted to forty-five dollars, having won twenty dollars from one of the boys, Ike Berry, on a horse race. They had a race horse in camp called "Gray-dog," who had never been beaten, so they said, but I and Whiskey-peat done him up, to the extent of twenty dollars, in fine shape.

I made up my mind that I would build me a "dugout" somewhere close to the Johnson camp and put in the winter hunting and trapping. Therefore as Hudson was going to Kiowa, with the wagon, after a load of provisions, etc., I went along to lay me in a supply also.

On arriving at Kiowa I found that my old "pard" Mr. Collier had struck a job with a cattleman whose ranch was close to town. But before spring he left for good "Hold Hengland" where a large pile of money was awaiting him; one of his rich relations had died and willed him everything he had. We suppose he is now putting on lots of "agony," if not dead, and telling his green countrymen of his hairbreadth escapes on the wild Texas plains.

After sending mother twenty dollars by registered mail and laying in a supply of corn, provisions, ammunition, etc., I pulled back to Eagle Chief, to make war with wild animals—especially those that their hides would bring me in some money, such as gray wolves, coyotes, wild cats, buffaloes and bears. I left Kiowa with just three dollars in money.

The next morning after arriving in camp I took my stuff and moved down the river about a mile to where I had already selected a spot for my winter quarters.

I worked like a turk all day long building me a house out of dry poles—covered with grass. In the north end I built a "sod" chimney and in the south end, left an opening for a door. When finished it lacked about two feet of being high enough for me to stand up straight.

It was almost dark and snowing terribly when I got finished and a fire burning in the low, Jim Crow fire-place. I then fed Whiskey-peat some corn and stepped out a few yards after an armful of good solid wood for morning. On getting about half an armful of wood gathered I heard something crackling and looking over my shoulder discovered my mansion in flames. I got there in time to save nearly everything in the shape of bedding, etc. Some of the grub, being next to the fire-place, was lost. I slept at Johnson's camp that night.

The next morning I went about two miles down the river and located another camp. This time I built a dug-out right on the bank of the stream, in a thick bunch of timber.

I made the dug-out in a curious shape; started in at the edge of the steep bank and dug a place six feet long, three deep and three wide, leaving the end next to the creek open for a door. I then commenced at the further end and dug another place same size in an opposite direction, which formed an "L." I then dug still another place, same size, straight out from the river which made the whole concern almost in the shape of a "Z." In the end furthest from the stream I made a fire-place by digging the earth away-in the shape of a regular fire-place. And then to make a chimney I dug a round hole, with the aid of a butcher knife, straight up as far as I could reach; then commencing at the top and connecting the two holes. The next thing was to make it "draw," and I did that by cutting and piling sods of dirt around the hole, until about two feet above the level.

I then proceeded to build a roof over my 3 x 18 mansion. To do that I cut green poles four feet long and laid them across the top, two or three inches apart. Then a layer of grass and finally, to finish it off, a foot of solid earth. She was then ready for business. My idea in making it so crooked was, to keep the indians, should any happen along at night, from seeing my fire. After getting established in my new quarters I put out quite a number of wolf baits and next morning in going to look at them found several dead wolves besides scores of skunks, etc. But they were frozen too stiff to skin, therefore I left them until a warmer day.

The next morning on crawling out to feed my horse I discovered it snowing terrible, accompanied with a piercing cold norther. I crawled back into my hole after making Whiskey-peat as comfortable as possible and remained there until late in the evening, when suddenly disturbed by a horny visitor.

It was three or four o'clock in the evening, while humped up before a blazing fire, thinking of days gone by, that all at once, before I had time to think, a large red steer came tumbling down head first, just missing me by a few inches. In traveling ahead of the storm the whole Johnson herd had passed right over me, but luckily only one broke through.

Talk about your ticklish places! That was truly one of them; a steer jammed in between me and daylight, and a hot fire roasting me by inches.

I tried to get up through the roof—it being only a foot above my head—but failed. Finally the old steer made a terrible struggle, just about the time I was fixing to turn my wicked soul over to the Lord, and I got a glimpse of daylight under his flanks. I made a dive for it and by tight squeezing I saved my life.

After getting out and shaking myself I made a vow that I would leave that God-forsaken country in less than twenty-four hours; and I did so.

The next morning after the steer racket I pulled out for Kiowa, Kansas. It was then sleeting from the north, consequently I had to face it.

About three o'clock in the evening I changed my notion and concluded to head for Texas. So I turned east, down the Eagle Chief, to where it emptied into the Cimeron, and thence down that stream; knowing that I was bound to strike the Chisholm trail—the one I came up on, the spring before.

I camped that night at the mouth of Eagle Chief and went to roost on an empty stomach, not having brought any grub with me. I was then in the western edge of what is known as the Black-jack country, which extends east far beyond the Chisholm trail.

The next morning I continued down the Cimeron, through Blackjack timber and sand hills. To avoid the sand hills, which appeared fewer on the opposite side, I undertook to cross the river, but bogged down in the quicksand and had to turn back.

That night I camped between two large sand hills and made my bed in a tall bunch of blue-stem grass. I went to bed as full as a tick, as I had just eaten a mule-eared rabbit, one I had slipped up onto and killed with a club. I was afraid to shoot at the large droves of deer and turkeys, on account of the country being full of fresh indian signs.

I crawled out of my nest next morning almost frozen. I built a roaring big fire on the *south* edge of the bunch of tall grass so as to check the cold piercing norther. After enjoying the warm fire a few moments, I began to get thirsty and there being no water near at hand, I took my tin cup and walked over to a large snow-drift a short distance off, to get it full of clean snow, which I intended melting by the fire to quench my burning thirst.

While filling the cup I heard a crackling noise behind me and looking over my shoulder discovered a blaze of fire twenty feet in the air and spreading at a terrible rate. I arrived on the scene just in time to save Whiskey-peat from a horrible death. He was tied to a tree, the top limbs of which were already in a blaze. I also managed to save my saddle and an old piece of saddle blanket, they being out under the tree that Whiskey-peat was tied to. I didn't mind losing my leather leggins, saddle blankets, etc., so much as I did the old delapidated overcoat that contained a little silver-plated match box in one of the pockets.

That day I traveled steady, but not making very rapid progress, on account of winding around sand hills, watching for indians and going around the heads of boggy sloughs. I was certain of striking the

Chisholm trail before night, but was doomed to disappointment.

I pitched camp about nine o'clock that night and played a single-handed game of freeze-out until morning, not having any matches to make a fire with.

I hadn't gone more than two miles next morning when I came across a camp-fire, which looked as though it had been used a few hours before; on examination I found it had been an indian camp, just vacated that morning. The trail, which contained the tracks of forty or fifty head of horses, led down the river. After warming myself I struck right out on their trail, being very cautious not to run onto them. Every now and then I would dismount and crawl to the top of a tall sand hill to see that the road was clear ahead.

About noon I came to a large creek, which proved to be "Turkey Creek." The reds had made a good crossing by digging the banks down and breaking the ice.

After crossing, I hadn't gone but a short distance when I came in sight of the Chisholm trail. I never was so glad to see anything before—unless it was the little streak of daylight under the steer's flanks.

The indians on striking the trail had struck south on it; and after crossing the Cimeron I came in sight of them, about five miles ahead of me. I rode slow so as to let them get out of sight. I didn't care to come in contact with them for fear they might want my horse and possibly my scalp.

About dark that evening I rode into a large camp of Government freighters, who informed me that the fifty indians who had just passed—being on their way back to the reservation—were Kiowas who had been on a hunting expedition.

I fared well that night, got a good supper and warm bed to sleep in—besides a good square meal of corn and oats for my horse.

The next morning before starting on my journey, an old irish teamster by the name of "Long Mike" presented me with a pair of pants—mine being almost in rags—and a blue soldier coat, which I can assure you I appreciated very much.

About dusk that evening, I rode into Cheyenne Agency and that night slept in a house for the first time since leaving Kiowa—in fact I hadn't seen a house since leaving Kiowa.

The next morning I continued south and that night put up at "Bill" Williams' ranch on the "South Canadian" river.

Shortly after leaving the Williams ranch next morning I met a crowd of Chickasaw indians who bantered me for a horse race. As Whiskey-peat was tired and foot-sore, I refused; but they kept after me until finally I took them up. I put up my saddle and pistol against one of their ponies. The pistol I kept buckled around me for fear they might try to swindle me. The saddle I put up and rode the race bareback. I came out ahead, but not enough to brag about. They gave up the pony without a murmer, but tried to persuade me to run against one of their other ponies, a much larger and finer looking one. I rode off thanking them very kindly for what they had already done for me.

The night I put up at a ranch on the Washita river and next morning before leaving swapped my indian pony off for another one and got ten dollars to-boot.

That morning I left the Chisholm trail and struck down the Washita river, in search of a good, lively place where I might put in the balance of the winter.

I landed in Erin Springs late that evening and found a grand ball in full bloom at Frank Murray's mansion. The dancers were a mixed crowd, the ladies being half-breeds and the men, mostly americans and very tough citizens.

Of course I joined the mob, being in search of excitement and had a gay old time drinking kill-me-quick whisky and swinging the pretty indian maidens.

After breakfast next morning the whole crowd, ladies and all, went down the river five miles to witness a ''big'' horse race at ''Kickapoo'' flat.

After the ''big race—which was for several thousand dollars—was over the day was spent in running pony races and drinking whisky. By night the whole mob were gloriously drunk, your humble servant included. There were several fights and fusses took place during the day, but no one seriously hurt.

It being against the laws of the United States to sell, or have whisky in the Indian territory, you might wonder where it came from: A man by the name of Bill Anderson—said to have been one of Quantrell's men during the war—did the selling.

He defied the United States marshalls and it was said that he had over a hundred indictments against him. He sold it at ten dollars a gallon, therefore you see he could afford to run quite a risk.

The next day on my way down the river to Paul's valley I got rid of my extra pony; I came across two apple peddlers who were on their way to Fort Sill with a load of apples and who had had the misfortune of losing one of their horses by death, the night before, thereby leaving them on the prairie helpless, unable to move on. They had no money to buy another horse with, having spent all their surplus wealth in Arkansas for the load of apples. When I gave them the pony, they felt very happy, judging from their actions. On taking my departure one of them insisted on my taking his silver watch as a token of friendship. I afterwards had the watch stolen from me.

The following May I landed in Gainesville, Texas, "right side up with care" and from there went to Saint Joe on the Chisholm trail, where I succeeded in getting a job with a passing herd belonging to Capt. Littlefield of Gonzales. The boss' name was "Jim" Wells and the herd contained thirty-five hundred head of stock cattle. It being a terribly wet season we experienced considerable hardships, swimming swollen streams, etc. We also had some trouble with indians.

We arrived in Dodge City, Kansas on the third day of July and that night I quit and went to town to "whoop 'em up Liza Jane."

I met an old friend that night by the name of "Wess" Adams and we both had a gay time, until towards morning when he got severely stabbed in a free-to-all fight.

On the morning of July fifth I hired to David T. Beals—or the firm of Bates & Beals, as the outfit was commonly called—to help drive a heard of steers, twenty-five hundred head, to the Panhandle of Texas, where he intended starting a new ranch.

The next morning we struck out on the "Old Fort Bascom" trail, in a southwesterly direction.

Gold is Where You Find it

The discovery of gold in any part of the West was always cause enough to send thousands flocking in that direction. The following passage comes from the journal of a young man from Ohio who left home with a group of friends to join the great California Gold Rush of 1849. What success did they have? How typical were their experiences? What made them keep trying? (H. L. Scamehorn, ed., The Buckeye Rovers in the Gold Rush *(1965), 119-33.)*

APRIL 28: Encamped on the North Fork of Middle Fork. Here we expect our home this summer. Last Tuesday three of us came to see some men Morrow and Buler were acquainted with. They told us we might get a claim next below theirs. We have it, and so far consider ourselves lucky. On this stream a person cannot hold more than one claim. This was claimed by a person who went in as a partner in a claim above. It is said to be very rich. We are situated one mile below the mouth of the Rich Canyon, yet we had to come four miles around. We now felt what it is to turn mule. We have packed three loads, some forty pounds each. The road is one that to be known must be seen, up one mountain and down one, two miles long and not less than five thousand feet high. Within some one thousand feet of the creek the trail is dug, winding from side to side, otherwise it would be almost impossible to travel it. Steep as it is, mules bring two hundred pounds down. On Tuesday we came down the canyon, some places where we crossed the bluffs made me tremble. One false step and all would be over. Death seemed suspended by a hair. The mountains are rugged and wild in the extreme.

MAY 5: A week of hard toil. We packed down our summer's provisions, each of us carrying fifty pounds on two days in succession. I have carried seven loads altogether down this mountain. The excitement about finding good diggings is wonderful. Men talk of getting gold by the pound. Went into the hills over the Eldorado Canyon, where we had been encamped, expecting some letters as some packers promised to be up from Sacramento and bring anything there might be in the office for us. Not up yet. Saw Bowers has a claim in Secret Canyon (so-named because many made fruitless efforts to find it). Says some New York men in a few weeks last fall dug ten thousand dollars each. He starts in the morning for Deer Creek dry diggins to work until the first of July. At present the snow in this canyon is from ten to thirty feet in depth. One place it is bridged with snow, though the stream is some thirty feet wide. In Deer Creek dry diggins some men last fall tied the legs of their pants to make sacks and carried off one hundred twenty-five pounds, so says Bowers. Other stories equally wild are told, seemingly in good faith. All are in wild excitement, or calmly waiting for the water to fall that they may jump and catch the gold.

MAY 12: This day spent in a way not the most agreeable. I attended a meeting of the miners of this district, which embraces all working on this river. The object of the meeting to elect an alcalde and make such regulations as might be thought advisable. Earlier in the season a similar meeting had been held when but few were on this stream. Now the cooperation of all was requested. Sunday is perhaps the only day men could be brought together. On this day but few work. Strange to witness, several men of intelligent appearance were loud in praise of mob law as more expeditious, more economical. In short, every way the best. This I opposed and had the pleasure to find a majority for what I deemed right. The meeting would compare favorably with some I have elsewhere seen. The path down the river to the place of meeting, some four miles, is on the side of the mountain, in many places one false step would precipitate a person many feet over rocks into the river. Wrote home this week and to Jane and Cornelius. Worked none. Weather somewhat cool. Snow not melting as fast as we wish. Heard considerable encouragement as to our prospect in mining. Received a letter from Jane and Cornelius.

MAY 19: The weather is delightful, the atmosphere dry and bracing. The middle of the day is as warm as midsummer in Ohio. Sometimes clouds appear and rain seems about to fall. One day the sun was surrounded by a very dark circle (one would say a very sure sign of rain), but in a short time nothing could be seen except a thickness, or milky appearance of the air like Indian Summer. We worked three days and made fifty dollars; small work for five. Drake was sick. The water begins to fall and the time for hard work drawing near.

MAY 26: Went up to Secret Canyon, went all around the heads of the Eldorado and within some thirty miles of the Sierra Nevada. Traveled many miles on snow one to five feet deep. Saw the snow bridge, but the stream is not more than one-half of thirty feet, almost impossible to walk through. Out three nights. Snowed and rained very hard for a time on Thursday. Frost every night. Could buy a claim for twenty-five dollars, fifty feet, but think best to confine ourselves to this. Appearance of gold good, but no certainty. Quartz in large quantities. Five with me, but one of our company. The snow is melting fast and yet there is some fifteen feet deep that I stood near. Three weeks since all the brush that we found so annoying was covered; snow then was five to ten feet on a level. On Thursday thunder and lightning, almost the only I have heard in California.

We walked on some ridges thousands of feet high, in some places so narrow two men could not go abreast. Mountains steep each side, but these mountains differ very much from the Rockies. There you see ranges principally of solid rock; here earth vastly predominates, making the mountains seldom precipitous. The prevailing rock here is slate, granite also, with seams of quartz. Saw but one deer and no other kind of game. Indians seem all gone from this region. Waters falling. All in good health.

JUNE 2: This time a year since we were pushing along Platte, straining every nerve to pass all teams near us. "Go ahead," our motto, little thinking what the latter part of the journey would be. Our ears were open for the least word relative to California. A year past and but little done. Thousands, I suppose, are now urging their way through mud and water, dust, and ashes for California, California. Men are getting to work in the Eldorado, and do not find it as rich as anticipated, yet there is too much water for a fair trial. Tomorrow we intend to commence to make plank for a part of our race. Got two axes ground; one dollar each for the use of a grindstone, two dollars for the use of a cross-cut saw per day, also two dollars for the use of a broad-axe per day, and sixteen dollars if it is injured. This is one way to make money.

For herding horses and mules, four dollars per week or fifteen dollars per month, and not accountable even at that. For bringing a letter from the city, two dollars and fifty cents, or one down, fifty cents. Satinette pants ten dollars, socks of poor quality one dollar fifty cents. Provisions on the same key; a fat ox two hundred dollars (some have been packed up and then killed), demand constant. Cheese a dollar fifty per pound, raisins the same, potatoes one dollar, and dried apples one dollar. Liquor plentiful at twenty-five cents per dram. I have not tasted the article in nearly three months.

The water has fallen some five inches in the last week. Dewing and

Earheart have been some time searching for a place to locate, but all is claimed. Some men have a half dozen or more claims, intending to speculate. A man told me he had been near the summit of the Sierra Nevada and that every place having the least appearance of gold was claimed. One individual perhaps claims one thousand feet of a stream, sticks up his notice "A.B. and Company (no telling how large that is) claim this stream up or down." Some places miners regulate this matter. On this stream, from its mouth to Eldorado, a company may take as much of this stream as they can drain. On the bars twenty feet square is all a man can claim; on Middle Fork but ten. The pretense of taking claims in the manner above described is to wait for low water, but at best it is only to try to be sure of the best. Decent men, to avoid strife, will respect them but others will not. It is somewhat amusing to see the poor fellows when they first arrive in the mines. How sadly disappointed they are; can't see a speck of gold what six or seven feet of dirt and rocks, and then not sure. O, if I had known this before I left home! You did not tell us of the thousands that make nothing. No, but you told us of the lumps. D--- such a country as this, if I can only get out, that's all!

JUNE 23: At this moment there is one of the most awful exhibitions of the affect of drunkeness that I have ever witnessed. A poor depraved mortal with a knife in his hand seeming to thirst for blood. O humanity, how art thou fallen! We were down to see Dewing, he has bought a share in a claim at one hundred fifty dollars, eight in the company. There is one of the most marvelous stories in circulation, even for this marvelous land. Some one hundred miles from here a lake has been discovered so rich as justly to entitle it to the name of Golden Lake. Fortunes are made in a few days. Thousands are flocking and, were I persuaded of its truth, of course I should be off. But Eldorado has failed, and Secret Canyon has lost its charm. All is not gold that glitters. My mind at times is tranquil and I feel as if certain of returning next winter; at other times I feel dejected, weary, and saddened. Our situation is exceedingly trying, waiting measurably on uncertainties.

JUNE 30: Another week and nothing made, but we have much hard work done on our race. Some one hundred feet is dug, and one hundred twenty feet of sleepers laid for boards which are ready. The sides are to be canvas. It cost one dollar per yard, nails seventy-five a pound, and tacks a dollar and a half a paper. Some are trying to turn the river, but there is three or four times too much water yet. Last Monday I received three letters, two carried by Dewing and Earheart, and one from Cornelius and Jane. All well. The middle of the day very warm.

JULY 4: Fourth of July, what do you bring to my memory as my mind dances back and forth on the wires of time? The past, where is it? In gloomy forgetfulness? No, but in the living present, treasured near my heart. The pleasure of the past invites me to happiness (its sorrows are but few). In the distance I see the Future, solemn but not sad, with outstretched arm she beckons me forward; Hope, with her golden wings and beautiful countenance, stands smiling at her side and I boldly advance. Thirty-two years on the road of life. Where am I? What am I? And what might I have been? Or what will a few more years unfold? These are questions I cannot answer now. For dinner today we ate peaches which grow on trees shading my home.

JULY 7: Went up the mountain seeking for letters. Found none. I have scarcely ever found a greater conflict of emotions. I feel almost overpowered by the intensity of the struggle: home and friends, deep anxiety, hope and fear, in quick succession. How little control we possess over our busy inmate who is constantly comparing the present with the past, or perhaps sketching out some pleasing view of the future, but ending with there is but little certainty there. Without hope of immortality what is life?

JULY 14: Received a letter from home. All in the enjoyment of good health. Wrote an answer, but how to get it to Sacramento I know not. The water is at last in our race. We have had nearly three months hard labor and next to no pay. Now that the time is near when we shall see the result, I feel as if a weighty lawsuit were pending and I am very fearful of the result. My only evidence is circumstantial.

JULY 21: How strange that nearly all our thoughts should be of gold. Yet circumstanced as we are, this is a comprehensive word. We are not misers, yet gold speaks of home, friends, and every near and endearing connection. If our prospects brighten we feel cheerful, our eyes dance in delight. On the other hand, when clouds cross our path, the storm and tempest rage within until the sunshine of hope dispels the gloom. We are now about half between hope and fear. Mr. Dewing was here, feels discouraged. He and I sent letters home. Most of the claims are now being tested and seem to prove possession not like pursuit. Above us Robinson and company are doing middling well. All must work in water.

JULY 27: Yesterday I received a very bad bruise on my left leg just below the knee. It is badly swelled, somewhat blackened, and very numb. It will prevent me from being able to work for some days. The bed of the river is a succession of large stones and rocks. As we roll them up in heaps, it requires caution. A man below had his foot broken by the fall of one. The rock that crushed against me would weigh more than a half a ton. I have employed myself since in making a shirt. I am a middling good tailor, but it puzzles me how women can live on the niggerdly wages they receive. Little wonder they seek to arouse the nation to a sense of their numerous wrongs. It is laughable to see men thrown on their own resources. Cooking in many cases is miserable, but patching takes the lead. Old boots, legs, canvas, flour sacks, no matter what and, as for know how, it is like the patches. The Amazonians got along well enough without men; Californians are trying the opposite experiment. For my part, I may pronounce it a complete failure. Today we joined claims with the company next below us. They had backed water on us so we could not work. They seemed willing to accomodate and we thought best to work theirs first. By this arrangement ten work together; four of Ohio, two of New York, two of Missouri, one of Illinois, and one of Virginia. Well mixed.

AUGUST 4: Perhaps there are few places more calculated more to try the mind than this. Except we possess some brace or support when our fancied-with is dashed away, we would be prostrate. Few exerted themselves more than we. I have been to Sacramento twice, less to Secret Canyon; out in the rain and snow, through mud, and over deep snow, and what have we—nothing but a severe lesson well learnt. At the present time we do not know that we shall have a cent. Some are leaving this stream, and all are more or less disappointed. The large streams, as a general thing, are best. Early in the season men thought there must be large deposits in the mountains and all the most enterprising were on the alert. Some crossed the Sierra Nevadas several times. In short, every place was tried. One man would think he found a rich place; others, learning of his secret, would magnify it, hence a rush. O here it is! O there it is! No mistake. How do you know? O, it was prospected last fall; two or three men took out ten or twenty thousand dollars then! Wait contented until the water falls. Presently all is claimed. Along comes a lot of poor fellows, well they are too late. See how disappointed they are. What a pleasant smile one side and a dejected frown on the other. He is forced to go back and content himself with some eight or ten dollars per day. Three or four months pass, how stands the balance now? He had one thousand dollars. We climb the mountain with a heavy heart and a light purse, some three or four hundred dollars worse than when the race began. Such is the history of many persons. Eldorado, Secret Canyon, South Fork of North Fork, North Fork of Middle Fork, perhaps not quite so bad yet bad enough. How many more I know not, these are all near. Some, however, find very good diggings. A Mr. Scott, keeping a store near us, won over one hundred dollars gambling today. Many, very many, will go home with long faces, very good men by the way and say, "see, I made one thousand dollars, I was industrious, I was fortunate, I had good diggings." Yes, you had gambling with drunken men. We intend to try this place a little longer. Lost four day's work, leg almost well.

AUGUST 11: No letters for us by this mail. We have a race four hundred eighty feet long in operation, yet our prospect is anything but encouraging. We joined interests with a company next below us. Their claim proved a failure, so we moved their canvas race. Very many are leaving this stream. Some claims prospected last fall and believed to be rich are being deserted. Ten of us made sixty-three dollars yesterday, poor pay in California.

Ranch Wife

Nannie Alderson as a bride went to live with her husband on a Montana cattle ranch in the 1870s. The following excerpt is taken from her autobiography. What differences were there between the labors of a pioneer woman and her counterpart in the settled regions? How did a new pioneer learn the work of the frontier? How would you characterize her daily life? Was there satisfaction in her work? Do you think she felt the same while she was living it as she did looking back forty years later? (N. T. Alderson and H. H. Smith, A Bride Goes West *(1942), 35-45.)*

The ignorance of brides has been a subject of jokes probably ever since the days of Mother Eve. My own ignorance as I look back upon it seems incredible—and like Eve I had to learn housekeeping in a wilderness. If I had married at home in West Virginia I should at least have had kindly neighbor women to turn to for advice, and I should have had stores where I could buy things to cover a few of my mistakes. As it was I was a hundred horse-and-buggy miles from a loaf of baker's bread or a paper of pins. And with one unpleasant pair of exceptions, I didn't see a white woman from April to July.

The exceptions, our only women neighbors, lived four miles away up Lame Deer Creek. My husband had told me about this family from Idaho who had moved in above us about a year before, and were running a few cattle. When they came there were a mother, father, and two sons, one of whom was married to a widow with three children, but the father had died the previous winter, and as my husband had the only lumber nearer than a hundred miles, he had furnished boards, made the coffin and helped bury the old man. He thought the women would feel kindly toward us and would, in any case, be glad to make a little extra money by doing our washing. So the first ride I took after reaching the ranch was to go and see this family and make arrangements.

When we rode up to their cabin the entire family trooped out to greet us. If I had expected a neighborly welcome, I found out I was mistaken. The mother was about six feet tall, dressed in a mother hubbard wrapper of calico with her late husband's straw hat on her head. She had iron grey hair cut squarely off on a line with the biggest ears I ever saw on any human, and her beady black eyes leveled on me with that "Well, what is your business?" expression that stops just short of hostility. The man looked like his mother but had a more kindly appearance. The daugher-in-law was a meek pale woman with two children clinging to her skirts, and throughout the interview she had nothing to say. It was plain that the older woman was the boss.

She eyed me from the top of my Eastern-made riding cap to the pointed toe of my boots, and I felt she was saying to herself: "This is a little fool, and she shall pay for it." When we told her we hoped she would do our washing, she said, boring holes in me with those beady eyes:

"You can furnish soap and starch, send the clothes up and Sadie will do the washing for ten cents apiece. We won't do the ironing at any price."

Feeling faint, I accepted. As Aunt Rose, our colored laundress down south, had done our entire family washing and ironing for years for five dollars a month, I felt that we were being robbed. I felt that way more than ever when the first bill was ten dollars and eighty cents. Clearly, our washerwoman would soon own our entire herd of cattle if I didn't learn to wash.

The next week when my husband was away on Tongue River buying horses I announced to the rest of the "family" that I was going to do the washing, and even invited the boys to put in their soiled things. I had never done a washing in my life and supposed, in my ignorance, that all it required was willing hands and soap. I knew nothing about hard water—but I soon learned.

For a guide to housekeeping in the West I had brought a cook book and housekeeping manual which our dear old pastor at home had given me for a wedding present. This book, written by a Southern gentlewoman for Southern gentlewomen, didn't contain a single cake recipe that called for fewer than six eggs. I now opened it to the section on laundry, and the first sentence that met my eye was as follows: "Before starting to wash it is essential to have a large, light, airy laundry with at least seven tubs."

I had one tub, a boiler and a dishpan. But for air and light at least I was well off, since my laundry was the shady north end of the shack and took in the whole of Montana. I threw the book under the bunk bed and put all my best clothes in the boiler. I didn't use half enough soap, and the water was very alkaline. My white under-things turned a dingy yellow and came out covered with gummy black balls of alkali as big as a small pea and bigger, which stuck to the iron. I shall never forget that washing as long as I live.

The boys did their best to help. One of them got dinner, and the others helped me to wring the clothes out of the hot water. I was grateful for their efforts and their sympathy, but as they didn't know any more about laundry than I did, it was a case of the blind leading the blind. I had so little sense, I didn't even know enough to pour cold water over the boiling clothes to cool them, and neither did the rest of them. We wrung them out hot, until my fingers were bleeding around the nails. There was no clothesline, so one of the boys stretched a lariat in the yard, but there were no clothespins either, and when a wind came up it blew down half of the wash into the sawdust which covered the premises. In the midst of all this Sadie, the neighbor's daughter-in-law, came to call, I think to find out why I hadn't sent the washing that week. Humiliation was forgotten in the relief of being able to sit down.

Back home in West Virginia I had thought myself quite a housewife. Mother was ill a great deal and I carried the keys, feeling very proud as I went about with her key basket, unlocking closets and giving things out. But out here I found that I didn't know, as they say, straight up. On the ranch we had meat without end, milk, and butter (if I made it), and later a few vegetables. Every single other necessity of life came from Miles City. Once a year when the men went in to ship their cattle they laid in supplies—hundred-pound sacks of flour and sugar, huge tins of Arbuckle coffee, sides of bacon, evaporated fruits and canned goods by the case. What you forgot you did without. I don't know how many times in those first months I thought: "Oh, if we'd only remembered" this or that.

We had plenty of canned corn and canned tomatoes, but the fruits were a luxury. Everyone in the country lived out of cans, and you would see a great heap of them outside of every little shack. But we always had a barrel for ours. I had to learn to cook and have a semblance of variety on the table with just what we had on hand. With no experience and no women to turn to, I don't know what I'd have done if it hadn't been for the friendly helpfulness of men.

I couldn't get over it. Back home, if we were without a cook, my stepfather would drive down into the colored section and hire a new one, but he wouldn't dream of going into the kitchen, even to carry a pail of water, and all the men were the same. But in Montana that first spring there would always be three or four in the kitchen getting a meal—Mr. Alderson, Mr. Zook, one of the cowboys and myself. I had Mr. Alderson's thoughtfulness to thank for this in the first instance, because they had been cooking before I came and he had warned them that they were not to cease doing their share. But they were very willing. I would often have to get a meal at odd hours, for one of our own boys or for a visitor who might arrive in the middle of the afternoon after riding fifty miles since breakfast. He'd be hungry and would have to be fed without waiting for supper, but I never got one of these extra meals without help. The men would always make the fire and grind the coffee and cut the meat, and would be so concerned about troubling me.

The boys taught me what they could. For instance, I learned from them how to make a very good rice pudding without any eggs. They would take the uncooked rice with a lot of raisins and currants and sugar and would cook it in milk, so long and slowly that it turned caramel-brown. They would mix it in a milk pan and set it in the oven, and every so often one of them would rush in from the corral where he was shoeing a horse or branding calves and stir it up.

As time went on I learned much from the roundup cooks who were out for months on end with the chuck wagons, and could turn out a delicious meal from a covered iron pot over an open fire.

These hardy Western men were nearly all bachelors, and so cooked in self-defense, but they did know how. It was one of them, a grizzled old cowboy, who taught me that the tops of young beets, which I'd been throwing away, make the most delicious of all greens. So when I went home to West Virginia the following year I introduced my grandmother to beet greens. When she tried them she said: "Well! To think that I've been keeping house for forty years, and it took a man to teach me about the best greens there are—and a man in Montana at that!"

My clothes were so inappropriate, they were ridiculous, though I never thought so at the time. They were just the ordinary clothes of a girl living in West Virginia. Nothing new was bought for my trousseau but my traveling dress, which was dark blue camel's hair with a velvet jacket. For the rest I had a black silk, a dark blue one with tiers of ruffles on the skirt, and a white poplin trimmed with broad black velvet bands. They all had trains, and I trailed them around over my dirt floors, which became very dusty as the summer wore on. There was no canvas spread in the kitchen, and the dust just couldn't be kept down, though I sprinkled it, and swept it, and even scooped it up with a shovel. I did pin up my skirts to work in, and I wore aprons, but still, nothing more glaringly impractical can be imagined. I had brought one half-way sensible dress, a blue serge, but the first of May we had a twelve-inch fall of snow one night. The sun came out and it promptly melted; the dirt roof leaked, and a rivulet of yellow mud ran down into the improvised clothes closet in one corner of our room, ruining that particular dress. After that I just wore what I had until I wore them out.

People have asked me, and I have wondered myself, why I didn't send to Miles City for a few yards of calico and make some plain washable clothes. The truth is it never occurred to me. The day of mail order catalogues hadn't arrived, and we were not in the habit of sending for things. Then too I have come to the conclusion that I was simply not very bright.

I can point with pride to only one piece of practical common sense —the use I made of my wedding veil. I remembered how as a girl in West Virginia I had seen my cousin Betty's veil, which she had kept put away in a box. The folds of silk tulle had simply stuck together and torn, when we tried to pull them apart so we could wear the veil in a pageant. I'd resolved then that if I ever had a wedding veil, I shouldn't be so foolish, but should get some good out of it. So in Montana I cut chunks out of mine and put it in folds around my neck.

The veil kept me reasonably fresh-looking, but there was no such thing as cleaning fluid, and of course dry cleaning establishments were unknown. I've often thought how untidy we must have been. There were no coat hangers—we hung our clothes on a nail. I had brought no shoe polish, because I never thought of it. We didn't do anything to scuff shoes in the South. But after a few weeks of steady wear on a ranch my black kid buttoned boots were a sight.

One morning shortly before I went to my first roundup, some

visitors arrived, among them Mr. Robinson, whose outfit was camped a few miles away, and who had ridden over to pay his respects to me. I saw the group of men ride up to the corral and dismount, and as I hurried to make myself presentable I wondered what to do about my shoes, which were shabby and foxy-red at the tips. Suddenly I remembered how as a child I had seen one of black Mammy's boys when getting ready to go to the village, turn up a black iron pot and take some of the soot to blacken his shoes. I seized a kettle and a rag and had just gotten the shabby spots covered when the visitors reached the house. I confessed what I had been doing and where I'd obtained my inspiration.

Mr. Robinson said: "Mrs. Alderson, you will get along all right on a cow ranch."

V. RIGHT AND WRONG

When the pioneers left their eastern homes and moved west they carried with them the standards of government, law, and morality to which they were accustomed. Often, however, their journey took them beyond the authority of the settled regions, and they had to rely on themselves to maintain those standards. How well did they succeed? What devices did they construct to order their new societies? What were the sources of their ideas of right and wrong? Did they imitate the systems and institutions they left behind, or construct entirely new ones? Did they view the measures they took as permanent or temporary? How do you think the lawyers, judges, lawmakers, and policemen of the settled areas felt about the way the pioneers handled their affairs.

Tennessee Politics

The famous David Crockett, in addition to his exploits as an Indian fighter and Texas revolutionary, was also active in the frontier politics of the Tennessee country in the 1810s and 1820s. The following is from a brief autobiography he wrote in the early 1830s. (David Crockett, Narrative of the Life of David Crockett . . . *(1834), 133-45.)*

The place on which I lived was sickly, and I was determined to leave it. I therefore set out the next fall to look at the country which had been purchased of the Chickasaw tribe of Indians. I went on to a place called Shoal Creek, about eighty miles from where I lived, and here again I got sick. I took the ague and fever, which I supposed was brought on my by camping out. I remained here for some time, as I was unable to go farther; and in that time, I became so well pleased with the country about there, that I resolved to settle in it. It was just only a little distance in the purchase, and no order had been established there; but I thought I could get along without order as well as any body else. And so I moved and settled myself down on the head of Shoal Creek. We remained here some two or three years, without any law at all; and so many bad characters began to flock in upon us, that we found it necessary to set up a sort of temporary government of our own. I don't mean that we made any president, and called him the "government," but we met and made what we called a corporation; and I reckon we called *it* wrong, for it wa'n't a bank, and hadn't any deposites; and now they call the bank a corporation. But be this as it may, we lived in the back-woods, and didn't profess to know much, and no doubt used many wrong words. But we met, and appointed magistrates and constables to keep order. We didn't fix any laws for them, tho'; for we supposed they would know law enough, whoever they might be; and so we left it to themselves to fix the laws.

I was appointed one of the magistrates; and when a man owed a debt, and wouldn't pay it, I and my constable ordered our warrant, and then he would take the man, and bring him before me for trial. I would give judgment against him, and then an order of an execution would easily scare the debt out of him. If any one was charged with marking his neighbour's hogs, or with stealing any thing, which happened pretty often in those days,—I would have taken, and if there was tolerable grounds for the charge, I would have him well whip'd and cleared. We kept this up till our Legislature added us to the white settlements in Giles county; and appointed magistrates by law, to organize matters in the parts where I lived. They appointed nearly every man a magistrate who had belonged to our corporation. I was then, of course, made a squire according to law; though now the honour rested more heavily on me than before. For, at first, whenever I told my constable, says I—"Catch that fellow, and bring him up for trial"—away he went, and the fellow must come, dead or alive; for we considered this a good warrant, though it was only in verbal writings. But after I was appointed by the assembly, they told me, my warrants must be in real writing, and signed; and that I must keep a book, and write my proceedings in it. This was a hard business on me, for I could just barely write my own name; but to do this, and write the warrants too, was at least a huckleberry over my persimmon. I had a pretty well informed constable, however; and he aided me very much in this business. Indeed I had so much confidence in him, that I told him, when we should happen to be out anywhere, and see that a warrant was necessary, and would have a good effect, he need'nt take the trouble to come all the way to me to get one, but he could just fill out one; and then on the trial I could correct the whole business if he had committed any error. In this way I got on pretty well, till by care and attention I improved my handwriting in such manner as to be able to prepare my warrants, and keep my record book, without much difficulty. My judgments were never appealed from, and if they had been they would have stuck like wax, as I gave my decisions on the principles of common justice and honesty between man and man, and relied on natural born sense, and not on law, learning to guide me; for I had never read a page in a law book in all my life.

About the time we were getting under good headway in our new government, a Capt. Matthews came to me and told me he was a candidate for the office of colonel of a regiment, and that I must run for first major in the same regiment. I objected to this, telling him that I thought I had done my share of fighting, and that I wanted nothing to do with military appointments.

He still insisted, until at last I agreed, and of course had every reason to calculate on his support in my election. He was an early settler in that country, and made rather more corn than the rest of us; and knowing it would afford him a good opportunity to electioneer a little, he made a great corn husking, and a great frolic, and gave a general treat, asking everybody over the whole country. Myself and my family were, of course, invited. When I got there, I found a very large collection of people, and some friend of mine soon informed me that the captain's son was going to offer against me for the office of major, which he had seemed so anxious for me to get. I cared nothing about the office, but it put my dander up high enough to see, that after he had pressed me so hard to offer, he was countenancing, if not encouraging, a secret plan to beat me. I took the old gentleman out, and asked him about it. He told me it was true his son was going to run as a candidate, and that he hated worse to run against me than any man in the county. I told him his son need give himself no uneasiness about that; that I shouldn't run against him for major, but against his daddy for colonel. He took me by the hand, and we went into the company. He then made a speech, and informed the people that I was his opponent. I mounted up for a speech too. I told the people the cause of my opposing him, remarking that as I had the whole family to run against any way, I was determined to levy on the head of the mess. When the time for the election came, his son was opposed by another man for major; and he and his daddy were both badly beaten. I just now began to take a rise, as in a little time I was asked to offer for the Legislature in the counties of Lawrence and Heckman.

I offered my name in the month of February, and started about the first of March with a drove of horses to the lower part of the state of North Carolina. This was in the year 1821, and I was gone upwards of three months. I returned, and set out electioneering, which was a bran-fire new business to me. It now became necessary that I should tell the people something about the government, and an eternal sight of other things that I knowed nothing more about than I did about Latin, and law, and such things as that. I have said before that in those days none of us called Gen'l. Jackson the government, nor did he seem in as fair a way to become so as I do now; but I knowed so little about it, that if any one had told me he was "the government," I should have believed it, for I had never read even a newspaper in my life, or any thing else, on the subject. But over all my difficulties, it seems to me I was born for luck, though it would be hard for any one to guess what sort. I will, however, explain that hereafter.

I went first into Heckman county, to see what I could do among the people as a candidate. Here they told me that they wanted to move their town nearer to the centre of the county, and I must come out in favour of it. There's no devil if I knowed what this meant, or how the town was to be moved; and so I kept dark, going on the identical same plan that I now find is called "*non-committal*." About this time there was a great squirrel hunt on Duck river, which was among my people. They were to hunt two days: then to meet and count the scalps, and have a big barbecue, and what might be called a tip-top country frolic. The dinner, and a general treat, was all to be paid for by the party having taken the fewest scalps. I joined one side, taking the place of one of the hunters, and got a gun ready for the hunt. I killed a great many squirrels, and when we counted scalps, my party was victorious.

The company had every thing to eat and drink that could be furnished in so new a country, and much fun and good humour prevailed. But before the regular frolic commenced, I mean the dancing, I was called on to make a speech as a candidate; which was a business I was as ignorant of as an outlandish negro.

A public document I had never seen, nor did I know there were such things; and how to begin I couldn't tell. I made many apologies, and tried to get off, for I know'd I had a man to run against who could speak prime, and I know'd, too, that I wa'n't able to shuffle and cut with him. He was there, and knowing my ignorance as well as I did myself, he also urged me to make a speech. The truth is, he thought my being a candidate was a mere matter of sport; and didn't think, for a moment, that he was in any danger from an ignorant back-woods bear hunter. But I found I couldn't get off, and so I determined just to go ahead, and leave it to chance what I should say. I got up and told the people, I reckoned they know'd what I come for, but if not, I could tell them. I had come for their votes, and if they didn't watch mighty close, I'd get them too. But the worst of all was, that I couldn't tell them any thing about government. I tried to speak about something, and I cared very little what, until I choaked up as bad as if my mouth had been jam'd and cram'd chock full of dry mush. There the people stood, listening all the while, with their eyes, mouths, and years all open, to catch every word I would speak.

At last I told them I was like a fellow I had heard of not long before. He was beating on the head of an empty barrel near the road-side, when a traveler, who was passing along, asked him what he was doing that for? The fellow replied, that there was some cider in that barrel a few days before, and he was trying to see if there was any then, but if there was he couldn't get at it. I told them that there had been a little bit of a speech in me a while ago, but I believed I couldn't get it out. They all roared out in a mighty laugh, and I told some other anecdotes, equally amusing to them, and believing I had them in a first-rate way, I quit and got down, thanking the people for their attention. But I took care to remark that I was as dry as a powder horn, and that I thought it was time for us all to wet our whistles a little; and so I put off to the liquor stand, and was followed by the greater part of the crowd.

I felt certain this was necessary, for I knowed my competitor could open government matters to them as easy as he pleased. He had, however, mighty few left to hear him, as I continued with the crowd, now and then taking a horn, and telling good humoured stories, till he was done speaking. I found I was good for the votes at the hunt, and when we broke up, I went on to the town of Vernon, which was the same they wanted me to move. Here they pressed me again on the subject, and I found I could get either party by agreeing with them. But I told them I didn't know whether it would be right or not, and so couldn't promise either way.

Their court commenced on the next Monday, as the barbacue was on a Saturday, and the candidates for governor and for Congress, as well as my competitor and myself, all attended.

The thought of having to make a speech made my knees feel mighty weak, and set my heart to fluttering almost as bad as my first love scrape with the Quaker's niece. But as good luck would have it, these big candidates spoke nearly all day, and when they quit, the people were worn out with fatigue, which afforded me a good apology for not discussing the government. But I listened mighty close to them, and was learning pretty fast about political matters. When they were all done, I got up and told some laughable story, and quit. I found I was safe in those parts, and so I went home, and didn't go back again till after the election was over. But to cut this matter short, I was elected, doubling my competitor, and nine votes over.

A short time after this, I was in Pulaski, where I met with Colonel Polk, now a member of Congress from Tennessee. He was at that time a member elected to the Legislature, as well as myself; and in a large company he said to me, "Well, colonel, I suppose we shall have a radical change of the judiciary at the next session of the Legislature." "Very likely, sir," says I, and I put out quicker, for I was afraid some one would ask me what the judiciary was; and if I knowed I wish I may be shot. I don't indeed believe I had ever before heard that there was any such thing in all nature; but still I was not willing that the people there should know how ignorant I was about it.

When the time for meeting of the Legislature arrived, I went on, and before I had been there long, I could have told what the judiciary was, and what the government was too; and many other things that I had known nothing about before.

The Hanging of George Ives

The gold camps of the West drew not only miners but men who preferred to let others dig for the gold and then take it away from them. In the Alder Gulch region of Montana during the 1860s, the community took the administration of justice into its own hands. In the following passage, the editor of the local newspaper describes the first of a long series of trials and executions. (Thomas J. Dimsdale, The Vigilantes of Montana *(1866), 103-15.)*

Tidings of the capture flew fast and far. Through every nook and dell of the inhabited parts of the Territory, wildly and widely spread the news. Johnny Gibbons, who afterwards made such sly and rapid tracks for Utah, haunted with visions of vigilance committees, joined the party before they reached the canyon at Alder Creek, and accompanied them to Nevada. At that time he was a part owner of the Cottonwood Ranch (Dempsey's), and kept the band well informed of all persons who passed with large sums of money.

The sun had sunk behind the hills when the detachment reached Nevada, on the evening of the 18th of December, and a discussion arose upon the question whether they should bring Ives to Virginia, or detain him for the night at Nevada. The "conservatives" and "radicals" had a long argument developing an "irrepressible conflict"; but the radicals, on a vote, carried their point—rejecting Johnny Gibbon's suffrage on the ground of mixed blood. It was thereupon determined to keep Ives at Nevada until morning, and then to determine the place of trial.

The prisoners were separated and chained. A strong guard was posted inside and outside of the house, and night came and went without developing anything remarkable. But all that weary night, a "solitary horseman might have been seen" galloping along the road at topmost speed, with frequent relays of horses, on his way to Bannack City. This was Lieutenant George Lane, alias Club-Foot, who was sent with news of the high-handed outrage that was being perpetrated in defiance of law, and with no regard whatever to the constituted authorities. He was also instructed to suggest that Plummer should come forthwith to Nevada, demand the culprit for the civil authorities, enforce that demand by what is as fitly called *hocus pocus* as *habaes corpus*, and see that he had a fair (?) trial.

As soon as it was determined that Ives should remain at Nevada, Gibbons dashed up the street to Virginia, meeting a lawyer or two on the way—

WHERE THE CARRION IS, THERE WILL THE VULTURES, ETC.

At the California Exchange, Gibbons found Messrs. Smith and Ritchie, and a consultation between client, attorney, and *proch ein ami*, resulted in Lane's mission to Bannack, as one piece of strategy that faintly promised the hope for rewards. All of Ives' friends were notified to be at Nevada early the next morning.

The forenoon of the 19th saw the still swelling tide of miners, merchants, and artisans wending their way to Nevada, and all the morning was spent in private examinations of the prisoners, and private consultations as to the best method of trial. Friends of the accused were found in all classes of society; many of them were assiduously at work to create a sentiment in his favor, while a large multitude were there, suspicious that the right man had been caught; and resolved, if such should prove to be the case, that no loophole of escape should be found for him, in any technical form of the law.

Although on the eve of "Forefathers' Day," there was in the atmosphere the mildness and the serenity of October. There was no snow and but little ice along the edges of sluggish streams; but the sun, bright and genial, warmed the clear air, and even thawed out the congealed mud in the middle of the streets. Little boys were at play in the streets, and fifteen hundred men stood in them, impatient for action, but waiting without a murmur, in order that everything might be done decently and in order.

Messrs. Smith, Ritchie, Thurmond, and Colonel Wood were Ives' lawyers, with whom was associated Mr. Alex Davis, then a comparative stranger in Montana.

Colonel W. F. Sanders, at that time residing at Bannack City, but temporarily sojourning at Virginia, was sent for to conduct the prosecution, and Hon. Charles S. Bagg was appointed his colleague, at the request of Judge Wilson, Mr. Bagg being a miner and then little known.

In settling upon the mode of trial, much difference of opinion was developed; but the miners finally determined that it should be held in the presence of the whole body of citizens, and reserved to themselves the ultimate decision of all questions; but lest something should escape their attention, and injustice thereby be done to the public, or to the prisoner, a delegation composed of twelve men from each district (Nevada and Junction) was appointed to hear the proof, and to act as an advisory jury. W. H. Patton, of Nevada, and W. Y. Pemberton, of Virginia, were appointed amanuenses. An attempt to get on the jury twelve men from Virginia was defeated, and, late in the afternoon, the trial began and continued till nightfall. The three prisoners, George Ives, George Hilderman, and Long John (John Franck), were chained with the lightest logging chain that could be found—this was wound round their legs, and the links were secured with padlocks. Opponents, recollect his actions with gratitude and kindly feeling. Charles S. Bagg is also remembered as having been at his post when the storm blew loudest.

The argument of the case having terminated, the issue was, in the first place, left to the decision of the twenty-four who had been selected for that purpose, and they thereupon retired to consult.

Judge Byam, who shouldered the responsibility of the whole proceeding, will never be forgotten by those in whose behalf he courted certain, deadly peril and probable death.

The jury were absent, deliberating on their verdict, but little less than half an hour, and on their return, twenty-three made a report that Ives was proven guilty; but one member—Henry Spivey —declined to give in any finding, for unknown reasons.

The crisis of the affair had now arrived. A motion was made, "That the report of the committee be received, and it discharged from further consideration of that case," which Mr. Thurmond opposed; but upon explanation, deferred pressing his objections until the motion should be made to adopt the report, and to accept the verdict of the Committee as the judgment of the people there assembled; and thus the first formal motion passed without opposition.

Before this, some of the crowd were clamorous for an adjournment, and now Ives' friends renewed the attempt; but it met with signal failure.

Another motion, "That the assembly adopt as their verdict the report of the Committee," was made, and called forth the irrepressible and indefatigable Thurmond and Colonel J. M. Wood; but it carried, there being probably not more than one hundred votes against it.

Here it was supposed by many that the proceedings would end for the present, and that the court would adjourn until the morrow, as it was already dark. Colonel Sanders, however, mounted the wagon, and having recited that Ives had been declared a murderer and a robber by the people there assembled, moved, "That George Ives be forthwith hung by the neck until he is dead"—a bold and business-like movement which excited feeble opposition, was carried before the defendant seemed to realize the situation; but a friend or two and some old acquaintances having gained admission to the circle within which Ives was guarded, to bid him farewell, awakened him to a sense of the condition in which he was placed, and culprit and counsel sought to defer the execution. Some of his ardent counsel shed tears, of which lachrymose effusions it is well to say no more than that they were copious. The vision of a long and scaly creature, inhabiting the Nile, rises before us in connection with this aqueous sympathy for an assassin. Quite a number of his old chums were, as Petroleum V. Nashby says, "weeping profoosly." Then came moving efforts to have the matter postponed until the coming morning, Ives giving assurances, upon his *honor,* that no attempt at rescue or escape would be made; but already Davis and Hereford were seeking a favorable spot for the execution.

Our Legislative Assembly seem to have forgotten that Mr. A. B. Davis had any of these arduous labors to perform, but none who were present will ever forget the fearless activity which he displayed all through those trials. A differently constituted body may yet sit in Montana, and vote him his five hundred dollars.

The appeals made by Ives and Thurmond for a delay of the execution were such as human weakness cannot well resist. It is most painful to be compelled to deny even a day's brief space, during which the criminal may write to mother and sister, and receive for himself such religious consolation as the most hardened desire, under such circumstances; but that body of men had come there deeply moved by repeated murders and robberies, and meant "business." The history of former trials was there more freshly and more deeply impressed upon the minds of men than it is now, and the result of indecision was before their eyes. The most touching appeal from Ives, as he held the hand of Colonel Sanders, lost its force when met by the witheringly sarcastic request of one of the crowd, "Ask him how long a time he gave the Dutchman." Letters were dictated by him and written by Thurmond. His will was made, in which the lawyers and his chums in iniquity were about equally remembered, to the entire exclusion of his mother and sisters in Wisconsin. Whether or not it was a time *for* tears, it was assuredly a time *of* tears; but neither weakness nor remorse moistened the eyes of Ives. He seemed neither haughty nor yet subdued; in fact, he was exactly imperturbable. From a place not more than ten yards from where he sat during the trial he was led to execution.

The prisoner had repeatedly declared that he would never "die in his boots," and he asked the sergeant of the guard for a pair of moccasins, which were given to him; but after a while he seemed to be chilled and requested that his boots might again be put on. Thus George Ives "died in his boots."

During the whole trial, the doubting, trembling, desperate friends of Ives exhausted human ingenuity to devise methods for his escape, trying intimidation, weak appeals to sympathy, and ever and anon exhibiting their abiding faith in "Nice, sharp quillets of the law." All the time the roughs awaited with a suspense of hourly increasing painfulness the arrival of their boasted chief, who had so long and so successfully sustained the three inimical characters of friend of their clan, friend of the people, and guardian of the laws.

Not more anxiously did the great captain at Waterloo sigh for "Night or Blucher" than did they for Plummer. But, relying upon him, they deferred all other expedients; and when the dreaded end came, as come it must, they felt that the tide in the affairs of villains had not been taken at its flood, and not without a struggle they yielded to the inevitable logic of events, and because they could not help it they gave their loved companion to the gallows.

Up to the very hour at which he was hanged they were confident of Plummer's arrival in time to save him. But events were transpiring throughout the Territory which produced intense excitement, and rumor on her thousand wings was ubiquitous in her journeying on absurd errands.

Before Lane reached Bannack, news of Ives' arrest had reached there, with the further story that the men of Alder Gulch were wild with excitement and ungovernable from passion; that a vigilance committee had been formed; a number of the best citizens hanged, and that from three hundred to five hundred men were on their way to Bannack City to hang Plummer, Ray, Stinson, George Chrisman, A. J. McDonald, and others.

Lane found Plummer anxious to look after his own safety rather than that of George Ives.

Ives' trial for murder, though not the first in the Territory, differed from any that had preceded it.

Before this memorable day, citizens, in the presence of a well-disciplined and numerous band of desperadoes, had spoken of their atrocities with bated breath; and witnesses upon their trail had testified in whispering humbleness. Prosecuting lawyers, too, had in their arguments often startled the public with such novel propositions, as, "Now, gentlemen, you have heard the witnesses, and it is for you to say whether the defendant is or is not guilty; if he is guilty you should say so, but if not, you ought to acquit him. I leave this with you, to whom it rightfully belongs." But the counsel for the defense were, at least, guiltless of uttering these last platitudes; for a vigorous defense hurt no one and won hosts of friends—of a *certain kind*. But on Ives' trial there was given forth no uncertain sound. Robbery and honesty locked horns for the mastery, each struggling for empire; and each stood by his banner until the contest ended—fully convinced of the importance of victory. Judge Byam remained by the prisoner from the time judgment was given, and gave all the necessary directions for carrying it into effect. Robert Hereford was the executive officer.

An unfinished house, having only the side-walls up, was chosen as the best place near at hand for carrying into effect the sentence of death. The preparations, though entirely sufficient, were both simple and brief. The butt of a forty-foot pole was planted inside the house at the foot of one of the walls, and the stick leaned over a cross beam. Near the point was tied the fatal cord with the open noose dangling fearfully at its lower end. A large goods box was the platform. The night had closed in with a bright, full moon, and around that altar of vengeance the stern and resolute faces of the guard were visible under all circumstances of light and shade conceivable. Unmistakable determination was expressed in every line of their bronzed and weather-beaten countenances.

George Ives was led to the scaffold in fifty-eight minutes from the time that his doom was fixed. A perfect Babel of voices saluted the movement. Every roof was covered, and cries of "Hang him!" "Don't hang him!" "Banish him!" "I'll shoot!" "—— their murdering souls!" "Let's hang Long John!" were heard all around. The revolvers could be seen flashing in the moonlight. The guard stood like a rock. They had heard the muttered threats of a rescue from the crowd, and with grim firmness—the characteristic of the miners when they mean "business"—they stood ready to beat them back. Woe to the mob that should surge against that living bulwark. They would have fallen as grass before the scythe.

As the prisoner stepped on to the fatal platform, the noise ceased, and the stillness became painful. The rope was adjusted, and the usual request was made as to whether he had anything to say. With a firm voice he replied, "I am innocent of *this* crime; Aleck Carter killed the Dutchman."

The strong emphasis on the word "this" convinced all around that he meant his words to convey the impression that he was guilty of other crimes. Up to this moment he had always accused Long John of the murder.

Ives expressed a wish to see Long John, and the crowd of sympathizers yelled in approbation; but the request was denied, for an attempt at a rescue was expected.

All being ready, the word was given to the guard, "Men, do your duty." The click of the locks rang sharply, and the pieces flashed in the moonlight as they came to the "aim." The box blew from under the murderer's feet with a crash, and George Ives swung in the night breeze, facing the pale moon that lighted up the scene of retributive justice.

As the vengeful click! click! of the locks sounded their note of deadly warning to the intended rescuers, the crowd stampeded in wild affright, rolling over one another in heaps, shrieking and howling with terror.

When the drop fell, the Judge, who was standing close beside Ives called out, "His neck is broken; he is dead."

This announcement and the certainty of its truth—for the prisoner never moved a limb—convinced the few resolute desperadoes who knew not fear, that the case was hopeless, and they retired with grinding teeth and with muttered curses issuing from their lips.

It is astonishing what a wonderful effect is produced upon an angry mob by the magic sound referred to. Hostile demonstrations are succeeded by a mad panic; rescuers turn their undivided attention to their own corporeal salvation; eyes that gleamed with anger roll wildly with terror; the desire for slaughter gives way to the fear of death, and courage hands the craven fear his sceptre of command. When a double-barreled shotgun is pointed at a traveller by a desperado, the feeling is equally intense; but its development is different. The organ of "acquisitiveness" is dormant; "combativeness" and "destructiveness" are inert; "caution" calls "benevolence" to do its duty; a very large lump rises into the wayfarer's throat; cold chills follow the downward course of the spine, and the value of money, as compared with that of bodily safety, instantly reaches the minimum point. Verily, "All that a man hath will he give for his life." We have often smiled at the fiery indignation of the great untried when listening to their account of what they would have done if a couple of road agents ordered them to throw up their hands; but they failed to do anything towards convincing us that they would have not sent valor to the rear at the first onset, and appeared as the very living and breathing impersonations of discretion. We felt certain that were they "loaded to the guards" with the gold dust, they would come out of the scrape as poor as Lazarus, and as mild and insinuating in demeanor as a Boston mamma with six marriageable daughters.

At last the deed was done. The law-abiding among the citizens breathed more freely, and all felt that the worst man in the community was dead—that the neck of crime was broken and that the reign of terror was ended.

The body of Ives was left hanging for an hour. At the expiration of this period of time it was cut down, carried into a wheelbarrow shop, and laid out on a work bench. A guard was then placed over it till morning, when the friends of the murderer had him decently interred. He lies in his narrow bed, near his victim—the murdered Tbalt—to await his final doom, when they shall stand face to face at the grand tribunal, where every man shall be rewarded according to his deeds.

Wagon Train Democracy

The pioneers who made up the wagon trains that passed over the Oregon Trail in the 1840s and 1850s came from all parts of the country and were strangers to each other at the start. The following passage describes the organization of one emigrant train in 1842. (Lansford W. Hastings, The Emigrants Guide to Oregon and California (1845), 4-9.)

The author long having had an anxious desire to visit those wild regions upon the great Pacific, which had now become the topic of conversation in every circle, and in reference to which, speculations both rational and irrational were everywhere in vogue, now determined to accomplish his desired object: for which purpose he repaired to Independence, Mo., which place was the known rendezvous of the Santa Fe traders, and the trappers of the Rocky mountains. Having arrived at Independence, he was so fortunate as to find, not only the Santa Fe traders, and the Rocky mountain trappers, but also a numer of emigrants, consisting of families and young men, who had convened there with the view of crossing the Rocky mountains, and were waiting very patiently until their number should be so increased as to afford protection and insure the safety of all, when they contemplated setting out together, for their favorite place of destination, Oregon territory. The number of emigrants continued to increase with such rapidity, that on the 15th day of May, our company consisted of one hundred and sixty persons, giving us a force of eighty armed men, which was thought ample for our protection. Having organized, and having ascertained that all had provided themselves with the necessary quantum of provisions and ammunition, as well as such teams and wagons as the company had previously determined to be essential, and indispensable, and all things else being in readiness, on the 16th day of May, in the year 1842, all as one man, united in interest, united in feeling, we were, *en route,* for the long desired *El Dorado* of the West.

Now, all was high glee, jocular hilarity, and happy anticipation, as we thus darted forward into the wild expanse, of the untrodden regions of the "western world." The harmony of feeling, the sameness of purpose, and the identity of interest, which here existed, seemed to indicate nothing but continued order, harmony and peace, amid all the trying scenes incident to our long and toilsome journey. But we had proceeded only a few days travel, from our native land of order and security, when the "American character" was fully exhibited. All appeared to be determined to govern, but not to be governed. Here we were, without law, without order, and without restraint; in a state of nature, amid the confused, revolving fragments of elementary society! Some were sad, while others were merry; and while the brave doubted, the timid trembled! Amid this confusion, it was suggested by our captain, that we "Call a halt," and pitch our tents, for the purpose of enacting a code of laws, for the future government of the company. The suggestion was promptly complied with, when all were required to appear in their legislative capacities. When thus convened, it was urged, by the captain, as a reason why we should enact a code of laws, that an individual of the party, had proposed to capture an Indian horse, and that he had made arrangements to accomplish his sinful purpose, by procuring a rope, and setting out with that view. In view of this alarming state of facts, it was urged by the over-legal and over-righteous, that the offending party should be immediately put upon his trial, for this enormous and wanton outrage upon Indian rights. This suggestion was also readily complied with, and the offender was soon arraigned, who, without interposing a plea to the jurisdiction, declared himself ready for trial, upon the "general issue." The investigation now commenced, during which, several speeches were delivered, abounding with severe and bitter denunciations of such highly criminal conduct, as that with which the prisoner at the bar of imaginary justice, stood charged. But it was urged on the part of the accused, that in whatever light his conduct might be viewed, by the advocates of "extreme right," it amounted to no crime at all; that to talk of taking an Indian horse, was neither *malum in se,* nor *malum prohibitum.* It was not criminal in itself, for in itself it was nothing, as he had *done* nothing. It was not criminal because prohibited, for in our infant state of society, we had no prohibitory code. The jury consisted of the whole company, who now with very little hesitancy, and almost unanimously, rendered their verdict of "not guilty," when the accused was discharged, and permitted to go hence, without day. Thus terminated the first jury trial, in our little community, whose government was extremely simple, yet purely democratic. This investigation, terminating as it did, afforded no valid reason for law-making, yet all being present with that view, and many being extremely anxious to accomplish the object for which they assembled, whether it was necessary or not, now proceeded to the discharge of the new, arduous and responsible duty of legislation. A committee was, therefore, appointed to draft a code of laws, for the future government of the company. This committee, contrary to the most sanguine expectations of the movers in this affair, reported that, in its opinion, no code of laws was requisite, other than the moral code, enacted by the Creator of the universe, and which is found recorded in the breast of every man. This report was adopted by an overwhelming majority, the consequence of which was, that no code of human laws was enacted; still there appeared to be a strong determination on the part of some, to do something in the way of legislating. In accordance with this determination, a decree was passed, which required the immediate and the indiscriminate extermination of the whole canine race, old and young, male and female, wherever they might be found, within our jurisdiction. This decree was passed by a very small majority, and it gave great dissatisfaction, especially to the owners of the animals whose extermination it contemplated. Those who favored its enforcement, insisted that the subjects of "the decree of death," however athletic they might be, could not possibly be taken through; that they would die before they had traveled half the distance; and that, by their incessant barking and howling, they would notify the Indians of our locality when encamped. On the other hand, it was insisted that, if they died on the way, that would be the loss of the owners, and, consequently, their business; and that if they did notify the Indians of our position, they would also notify us of theirs; and hence, the conclusion was drawn, that the advantages more than counterbalanced the disadvantages. Notwithstanding this conclusion, several dogs were slain under the inconsiderate decree, when the opposition became more general and determined. The owners of the most valuable mastiffs now declared in the most positive terms, that "if any man should kill their dogs, they would kill him, regardless of all consequences." The "dog killers," however, now went out "armed and equipped," as the decree required, with a full determination to discharge their *honorable* and *dangerous* duty; but they were promptly met by the owners, who were also "armed and equipped," and prepared for any emergency. At this important crisis, the captain thought proper to convene the company again, in its legislative capacity, which being done, the "dog decree," as it was called, was almost unanimously abrogated. This was our first and last effort at legislation. This legislative rebuff, however, was not the only difficulty which we here encountered.

Our misfortunes were heightened by disease and death. The wife and child of a Mr. Lancaster were taken very ill, and the child soon died. Mrs. Lancaster remained very low for several days, during which time, the company remained in camp; but as there were no prospects of her immediate recovery, and as any considerable delay in this section, might be attended with fatal consequences to the whole company, Mr. Lancaster determined to return to the States, which he could very safely do, as we were but a few days travel from the Missouri line, and as we had passed no hostile Indians. Upon arriving at this determination, we continued our journey, and Mr. Lancaster returned to the States, where he safely arrived, as I have since learned. We passed on now very agreeably, with the exception of the occasional expression of dissatisfaction with our officers, which, however well founded, grated harshly upon the ears of the order-observing, and law-abiding portion of the company. In a very few days, we met a company of traders from Fort Larimie, on their way to the States, with their returns of furs and buffalo robes, which they had accumulated during the previous year. These furs and robes were transported in wagons, drawn by oxen. Here many of our party for the first time, saw the buffalo. The only ones, however, which they saw here, were eight or ten buffalo calves, which the traders had domesticated for the St. Louis market; and so completely domesticated were they, that they followed the cows, which had been taken out for that purpose, with very little trouble to the drivers. This meeting afforded a very favorable opportunity for forwarding letters to the States, of which many of the party were happy to avail themselves.

By this time, the party had become greatly incensed with the officers, and had determined upon holding an election, for the purpose of electing other officers. Accordingly an election was held, which resulted in the election of myself to the first, and a Mr. Lovejoy to the second office of our infant *republic*. This election gave some dissatisfaction, to a few of the party, especially the disaffected and disappointed office-holders and office-seekers, who now, together with a few others, separated themselves from the main body, and went on a few days in advance, to Fort Larimie, where they had been but a few days, when the main body arrived. Upon arriving at Forts Larimie and John, we were received in a very kind and friendly manner by the gentlemen of those forts, who extended every attention to us, while we remained in their vicinity. While here several of our party disposed of their oxen and wagons, taking horses in exchange. This they were induced to do, under the impression that their wagons could not be taken to Oregon, of which they were assured by the gentlemen of those forts, and other mountaineers. Many others of the party, disposed of their cows and other cattle, which had become tender footed, as from this cause, it was supposed, that they would soon, be unable to travel; but we found by experience, that by continued driving, their hoofs became more and more hardened, until they had entirely recovered. Before leaving these forts, the disaffected of our party, proposed to unite their destinies again with ours; but the main body being so exasperated with their former course, for some time refused their consent, yet in view of the fact, that they must either travel with us, remain at these forts, or return to the States, they were permitted to join us again, when, we were once more, enabled to continue our toilsome, yet interesting journey.

Leaving these forts, we had traveled but a few miles, when we met a company of trappers and traders, from Fort Hall, on their way to the States, among whom was a Mr. Fitspateric, who joined our party, as a guide, and traveled with us, as such, to Green river. From this gentleman's long residence in the great western prairies, and the Rocky mountains, he is eminently qualified as a guide, of which fact, we were fully convinced, from the many advantages which we derived from his valuable services. He was employed by Dr. White, who had received the appointment of Indian agent of Oregon, and who was under the impression, that our government would defray all such expenses; which impression however, I think, was entirely unfounded. Perfect unanimity of feeling and purpose, now having been fully restored, we passed on very agreeably.

Incest and Fratricide

The harshness and isolation of pioneer life sometimes set the stage for acts of madness and violence. In the incident described below, which crime did the community feel worse, the son's or the father's? What does the episode reveal about the moral qualities of the community? The time and place was Idaho in the 1890s. (N. P. Greenwood, We Sagebrush Folks, *288-90.)*

The whole country-side was shocked by the news that Old Man Branch had been murdered by his fifteen-year-old son Reffie—short for Ralph. Shot in the head, he was, with his own gun. His brains were shot out, and he was still gripping the green onion he was eating when they moved his body away from the table. Folks said they were not surprised. That Reffie Branch was too quiet to come to any good. He always acted like he was trying to keep away from folks.

I know now that the boy was living in hell, and when you are living in hell, you cannot be very sociable with other people. Old Man Branch was a brutal slave-driver; no one could doubt that who once saw that subdued family when he was near. We had very little chance to see them, for he kept them there on his isolated farm, working day and part of the night. They never came to our good times.

There was a girl older than Reffie, a pretty, rounded girl with lovely brown hair and dark eyes. She was very shy and modest. Besides this girl and Reffie, there were seven younger children.

One day Reffie was about to plow, when he noticed that one of the cows was missing from the piece of pasture-land. He crossed the field, looking for it, and instead found his mother, groaning and sobbing behind a strawstack. She had come there feeling certain of secrecy.

Reffie demanded the reason of her tears, and at last she told him.

The story came out at the trial, just as she had related it to him. Betty, the eldest girl, was in the habit of collecting the eggs from the barn in the evening after supper. One night she found her father there. He seized her, caressed her with ferocity, and finally, there on the hay, her own father forced the poor child of barely seventeen years. He threatened to kill her if she told any one, and he commanded her to return every evening. He also formed the habit of bringing her little cheap presents from town—beads, rayon hose, and such. The poor mother had been glad at this manifestation of affection.

Reffie was crying, too, when the story was done. And he was swearing— "Damn him! . . . damn him! . . . God and Jesus Christ damn him!" Then he said to his mother, "Don't cry no more, Ma. It don't make no mind. I should ought to of killed him long ago. He'll get his come-uppances."

His mother hardly heard him. What could a fifteen-year-old boy do to right this horrible affair? She dragged herself up from the straw some time afterward. It was time enough for Reffie to go to the house, get his father's shot-gun, secrete it under the door-step, and begin his plowing. The lost cow had strayed back to the pasture while he was with his Ma.

That night he made no move to come in from the field until his father shouted in exasperation from the kitchen door. Then he took his time, unharnessing deliberately, knotting up the straps, and leading the horses to the canal with the ends dangling. There is nothing more peaceful than the sound of horses drawing up great soughing mouthfuls of water in the quiet of a desert evening. Reffie was not thinking of that. He was remembering now how his sister Betty's body had changed . . . he knew now . . . she was going to have a baby . . . her own father . . .

He pitchforked a mangerful of hay to the horses and left them contently *chawnking* as he slipped stealthily around the back of the house and carefully surveyed the kitchen through the extreme side of the open window. There was no screen. It had been one of those hot days in spring which nature means as a warning of summer's coming. The family were all eating, his father's great back toward the window.

Dragging the gun lightly from under the step, Reffie placed it on the window-ledge, took careful aim, and fired. Brains all over; family screaming and scrambling; green onion gripped in the old devil's hand.

Reffie jumped on the bay mare and rode to town, where he gave himself up. The trial was very brief. He was acquitted.

VI. HEAVEN AND EARTH

When the pioneers moved west they did not leave their religion behind, and churches were founded in most areas as soon as settlement. How important was religion to the pioneers? How much time did they devote to church? Do you think people on the frontier were more or less concerned with matters of religion than their contemporaries in the settled regions? Why? Did the frontier church play any other role in the community than the purely religious? Did the church involve itself in matters which today we would think were not its business? How closely connected was the frontier church to neighboring churches and to established church associations in the settled regions? Can you tell if pioneer churches were more or less formally organized than pioneer governments? How important was the minister to frontier religion? How was he chosen? What were the limits of his authority?

*

The Early Years of a Frontier Church

Settlement of west-central Illinois began along the bottoms of the Mississippi River in the 1820s, and churches were established from the start. The following passage is excerpted from the records of one of the oldest still in existence. (First Baptist Church of Barry, Illinois, Manuscript Records, Vol. I, 1-46.)

We the united Baptist Church of Christ Convene at Atlas on the 3rd Saturday in June 1829 Covenant and believe in the following doctrins of the gospel viz

1st We believe there is one God the father the word and the Holy Ghost and these three are one

2nd   We believe that the old and new testaments are the word of God and the only rule of faith and practice

3rd   We believe that all men are Sinners for Sin hath entered in to the world and death by Sin and so death has passed upon all men for that all hath Sined

4th   We believe that Salvation is offered by the life death and resurection and asension and advocacy of Jesus Christ who is exalted a promise and a Savior to give repentance and remission of Sins and hath commanded all men and everywhere to repent

5th   We believe that Sinners are Justified in the Light of God by the righteousness of Christ imputed to them which is unto and upon all that believe

6th   We believe that such are the Isrealites indeed and the Sheep of Christ to them he gives eternal life and they shall never perish and that these are the only proper subjects of Baptism and that baptism is emersion that they shall be Careful to maintain good works which are the evidence of faith

7th   We believe that Baptism and the Lord's Supper are appointed by Jesus Christ and should be attended by believers only

8th   We believe that God has appointed a day in which he will Judge the world in righteousness and there shall be a resurection of the bodies of the Just & unjust and the wicked shall go away into ever lasting punishment but the righteous into life eternal

9th   We believe that no minister have a right to the administration of the Sacred ordinances but Such as profess pure Principles and have gone under the hands of the presbytery and we are to Judge by hearing them and these are to live of the gospel

10th   We believe that it is our duty to be kind and affectionate to each other and aid the happiness and prosperity of the Children of God in general and endeavor to keep up a union and communion and correspondence with sister Churches

On the above abstract of principles and Constitution of the members of the said Church we the undersigned elders do Constitute a united Baptist Church of Christ in the name of the father and of the Son and of the Holy ghost.

Jacob Bowers
Jesse Sutton

We the members of the aforesaid Church do for our better regulation and to keep our house in order establish the following rules of decorum to wit

1st The Church shall meet on the Saturday before the fourth Sabbath in each month at some house near Kysis Creek in the precinct of Pleasant Vale at 11 O'clock A. M. to do and transact all business in any wise pertaining to the Church and to continue etc---

2nd The pastor of the Church shall be the moderator in his absence the brethern Shall appoint some one of their number by a majority of votes to act as their moderator or the brethern may at any or these said meetings appoint their moderator if proper

3rd It shall be the duty of the moderator to cause the meeting to be opened and closed with prayer and singing and when opened to proceed to business

4th There shall be chosen some suitable brother from among the members to serve as Clerk of the Church whose duty it shall be to keep in a book furnished him by the Church the regular proceedings and transactions of said Church also to keep a list of the names of all the members of said Church the manner of admission whether by letter or experience to give letters of dismissal when ordered by the Church to keep an account of the numbers of deaths exclusions etc

5th Every motion made and seconded shall be attended to unless withdrawn by the person who made it and no amendment shall be made unless approved by the person making the motion

6th Only one person shall speak at a time whose duty it shall be to rise from his seat and address the moderator and the person speaking shall not be interrupted so long as he tends to the subject under consideration but shall not speak more than three times to the same point or subject without leave from the Church

Minister to the Frontier

Orceneth Fisher spent his life preaching on the frontier as it moved westward. In the following letter, he explained his motivations and beliefs to a younger minister. (W. Warren Sweet, ed., Religion on the American Frontier *(1946), II, 470-79.)*

Corvallis, Oregon. Nov. 16, 1860

Rev. J. Spencer.

DEAR BROTHER,

In brief reply to your inquiry, I state

1*st* I was born in the town of Chester, Vt. Nov. 5, 1803. My parents, Dr. David and Britania Fisher were both of the Baptist Church, rather Free Will Baptist in their belief.

2*d* Of course I was not baptised in my infancy, which was a grievous stumbling block to me when I began to feel my own personal responsibility before God.

3 My early religious impressions were very early, perhaps about my seventh year. When I was about twelve years old my mother encouraged me to undertake the reading of the Bible through by course. This I did, and soon became interested in the contents; but when I came to the history of Abraham and read the terms of the covenant God made with him, and through him with all the world and sealed it with circumscision, I saw at once in the clearness of sun light, that the Gospel was the development of this great Covenant, and that Baptism now stood to men in the same relation that circumscision had formerly done, and as I was unbaptised, I was terribly afraid I was left out of the mercy of God altogether and my damnation sealed. Words cannot explain the trouble I endured on this account. I went to my mother in the anguish of my heart, but all in vain; she could give me little comfort by telling me that "Infant baptism was only a *human* invention!" etc. This very much discouraged my Bible reading; however, I still read the Bible occasionally, but tried to forget my fears and trouble as best I could. I was trained to fear God, to revere his name; to regard his Sabbath, though not so sacredly as, I think, I should have been. A little too much looseness in this department of my education, let me slide into bad company, where I was in great danger of learning bad habits. But by the mercy of God, his fear [illegible] from me. I never used His name profanely from the time I was old enough to know the import. I maintained a pretty fair morality; knowing however all the time that I must be born again or never inter [enter] into the Kingdom of God.

4 When between 11 and 17 years of age I was deeply convinced of my danger as a sinner in the sight of God, and especially as a *neglector* of the great Salvation. This conviction was the direct work of the

Spirit of God upon my heart while at work by myself in the field. Such a flood of light all at once, (while I was musing) poured into me as fully revealed to me what I was w[h]ither I was going, and what must be the fearful consequences if I still refused to be reconciled to God! I stood amazed, confounded, bewildered, and greatly terrified. I could not work, I could scarcely see for a time! I saw my former resolutions had been forgotten, God had been neglected, and I was taking the broad road to hell, or was at least about to do it. I tremble[d] in myself, and resolved to give myself to God at once and enter into his service. But such was my ignorance of the plan of salvation, and so unwilling was I that anyone should know that I was becoming religious, that it was several months before I felt any evidence of my acceptance with God, or any special encouragement in seeking him.

5 Having one day been discovered at secret prayer in the woods by three men who rode by me on horseback, I concluded it was useless to attempt longer to conceal my religious purposes, and began to converse on the subject with some religious friends who were Methodists. I soon found the benefit of this; they had gone that way before me and could tell much about it. Seeing the members of the church pray in their Prayer meeting, and seeing a friend of mine take up the cross and pray before he joined the church, I thought I must do so too. This was, however, a heavy cross, and the pain of it almost equal to the pain of sin. I perferred it however to the latter, and after. . . .

[The next two pages of the manuscript are lost.]

My father of blessed memory, who had been firm in opposing me as a Methodist, up to this time, now entirely relaxed, changed his behaviour toward me, acknowledged his wrong, gave me liberty to go when and where I should think best to call sinners to repentance, and bid me God speed in the work! It came like a revelation from heaven! I took solemn leave of home to go out into the wide western world, I knew not whither, not doubting that God had a place for me some where in his vast heritage.

In Smith's Settlement [Dearborn County] about seven miles from home I spent about a week. It was Christmas time [1822]. I could not pass my old friends and brethren without holding a meeting with them, and having held [one], another foll[o]wed as a matter almost

of necessity, and another, and another, until the week was gone! and
a glorious one it was. My own soul overflowed with the love of God
incessantly day and night. Sometimes in walking out by myself my
soul was so filled with the love of God that it seemed impossible to
keep from shouting at the top of my voice.

The church was greatly revived during my stay here, and it was exceedingly difficult to get away from these holy and loving people.
Some thought I was doing wrong to leave them. And after I had torn
myself away and was gone this thing was for a short time a temptation to me, lest I disregard the voice of Providence in this matter; but
having laid the whole subject before God in solemn prayer with an
earnest desire to know his will and with a fixed determination by his
grace to do it, the cloud soon passed away and I felt a sweet
assurance within that I was in the path of duty. A few days ride
brought me into the neighborhood of the camp ground where I had
been in the summer before, the north end of the Charlestown circuit,
Mo. Conference, Jas. Armstrong preacher in charge. Here I met with
some acquaintances, and as I had a letter of introduction from Alexander Cummings, P. E. and W. L. Draper and Wm. Lambden, preachers of the Lawrenceburg circuit, to Sam'l Hamilton, P. E. of Indiana
District of the Mo. Conference, I determined to wait the coming of
the preachers on the circuit by whom I would find the whereabouts
of the P. E. In the meantime I was holding family, social, and general
Prayer meetings, and God was with us in awakening and converting
power. The day the preacher was to come I went to his meeting, but
he was late, and the people insisted I should preach, so, tremblingly I
went at it, looking every moment for the preacher, but God was with
us, owned his word in power, and many hearts were deeply moved.
When about two-thirds through my discourse, the preacher came and
another with him. I closed rather abruptly to give place to him. He
attempted to hold classmeeting, but so powerful was the work of God
on the hearts of sinners and saints that some were crying aloud for
mercy, and other[s] shouting for joy. Two were clearly converted.

Bro. Armstrong decided that I should remain with him until his
Quarterly Meeting, (about 6 or 8 weeks) and that then he would have
me employed with him by the Elder. We labored together a few days.
At a night appointment bro. A. put me up to preach. 4 were converted. He preached the next night and 9 were converted. But soon

bro. A. said I must take my own appointments, two weeks after him around the circuit. At the Quarterly Meeting, Bro. Hamilton the P. E. received me and sent me to Vincenns circuit, to supply the place of I. Ingersol, who had declined taking the work. This was another trial. About 80 had joined the church during my stay here, and I had become warmly attached to many and they as warmly attached to me. But duty had to be done and there was no time for parting. I arrived on the circuit on the 3d of March,1823. It extended from Vincennes to the vicinity of Old Fort Harrision, up the Wabash river, and east into the forks of White River and up the east fork to Mt. Pleasant and above—and across the west fork near Black Creek.

The circuit had been a considerable time without a preacher and was in consequence much dilapedated; I had no plan of it, and was under the necessity of hunting up the preaching places as best I could, these were sometimes far apart, and some times there were no roads, or next to none, and sometimes neither bridges nor ferries. In the spring the waters were high, and sometimes my boat was my horse, upon whom I made some serious adventures, through deep wide and rapid streams, with the water near the freezing point. One day in crossing the west fork of White river, I was in the water fording sometimes over my horse's back and sometimes swimming for about the day. But, thanks be to God, came out unharmed without the use of brandy, or any other stimulant then [than] the love of God and natural plain food.

I was on this work about seven months; filled, I believe about 26 or 28 appointments in four weeks; often preaching day and night besides holding class and Prayermeetings. Three hundred and eighteen were added to the church during that time, (a very few by letter) making about 400, who had joined the church on both circuits where I had labored.

Rev. Job M. Baker, and several local preachers aided me on this circuit. One of the latter, Rev. John Miller, has since won a reputation as a travelling preacher. Quite a number of the converts on this circuit afterwards entered the ministry.

At the next session of the conference, which was held in St. Louis, I was received on trial and appointed to the Illinois circuit, including the towns of Bellville, Lebanon, Edwardsville, and Alton, and their vicinities, Rev. Jno. Dew, in charge, and Rev. S. H. Thompson, P. E.

on this circuit, we had a good work and about 150 accessions to the church. Some of these became ministers, among whom was Rev. Smith L. Robinson, who served the church with great efficiency a few years, and fell at his post full of holy honors. Next year I formed the Boon[s]ville circuit, Indiana. About two hundred were added to the church, among whom was Dr. A. Talbot, who became a distinguished minister. My next appointment was Mt. Vernon Circuit, Illinois. Here we had a good work, but in the midst of it my health (which had been failing for years under my severe labors and exposure to the severe cold of the prairies in the winter,) so far gave way that I was compelled to rest. I did not again permanently resume the regular work until 1837, but as my health and strength admitted I labored far and nigh, holding camp, two-days, and other meetings, and administering baptism to hundreds (as well as the Lord's Supper) where there were no ordained ministers to do those things. In this way I often supplied the place of a presiding elder over a large extent of country. My residence was the greater part of the time in Nashville, Illinois. I believe there are few traveling preachers now who do more work than I did then, and all without fee or reward, save in a few instances, and as I had a rising family, and was myself without means it was absolutely necessary that I should labor with my own hands for my own family's support. And as the country was new, and the climate rigorous in winter, and sickly in summer, my labors were often very heavy. In 1837, I resumed the regular work and was stationed in Carlyle, the next two years on the Waterloo circuit, and in 1840 in Springfield. In all these places God was with us, and good was done. On Waterloo 1839 we had a glorious work, but here I fell again by sickness right in the midst of a glorious revival. In the winter of 1839-40, I visited Texas, and in 1841 received a regular transfer to that work, where I remained until the spring of 1855. My last 5 appointments in Texas were on Districts in East Texas. Prior to that I had labored in the Texas Conference; three years in Houston City, where I started and edited and published the Texas Christian Advocate for the first year. During my stay of 14 years in Texas God was with us, often in great power and thousands were added to the church; about 2400 on the several districts I traveled in East Texas. I could report many instances of divine power of the most thrilling character, but it would make this article too long.

In 1855 I was transferred to the Pacific Conference, in which I still labor. My appointments have been San Francisco, 1855, Stockton, 1856-7. San Francisco District 1858-59. Oregon District 1860-61. During my second year I edited and pu[blished the *Pacific Methodist*, which still] lives and flourishes under the editorial skill of Rev. O. P. Fitzgerald. God has given me many souls in California and Oregon. And as in my former fields of labor, so here, some have already entered the ministry and are bringing other[s] to God.

Oregon is a new field of labor for Southern Methodists, where we meet with a good deal of opposition, and yet also of encouragement. We have already between 300, and 400 members, and hope for a rich harvest. It will be seen by the preceeding narative that I have been in the main a frontier man. Of course I have not enjoyed those facilities for acquiring literature that those who have remained among the Colleges and Libraries have enjoyed. Still I have made some acquaintances with the Hebrew and Greek Languages, and have written and published several works, one on Baptism and the Lord's Supper and the History of Immersion, a large octavo, which has received the approval of several of our Bishops, and several of our conferences, besides the commendation of several distinguished and learned ministers of other denominations; among whom I have the pleasure of naming W A. Scott D. D. of the Presbyterian Church, San Francisco, Cal. I could say much more, but perhaps I have already drawn out these sketches too far. My purpose is still to work for God while I live. I have suffered much in the flesh with several courses of fever in Illinois which reduced me to a mere skeleton of skin and bone, with a deep consumption and yellow fever in Texas, have had my bones broken, spine erreparantly [*sic*]; have been several times reported dead, and yet thank God, I am alive and so labor more in the ministry than any man of my acquaintance, To God be all the glory Amen. I hope to preach the gospel in Mexico before I die.

O. FISHER

Revivals and Camp Meetings

Religious services often served as an emotional release for frustrations built up by the hardships of frontier life. This was true for those who scoffed at religion as well as those who believed in it. Peter Cartwright, a circuit-riding Methodist preacher, was prominent in early religious activities on the Midwestern frontier. In the following passages he describes some of his experiences on the Tennessee and later Illinois frontiers. (Autobiography of Peter Cartwright, *Cincinnati, 1860, 43-49, 232-35.*)

From 1801 for years a blessed revival of religion spread through almost the entire inhabited parts of the West, Kentucky, Tennessee, the Carolinas, and many other parts, especially through the Cumberland country, which was so called from the Cumberland River, which headed and mounted in Kentucky, but in its great bend circled south through Tennessee, near Nashville. The Presbyterians and Methodists in a great measure united in this work, met together, prayed together, and preached together.

In this revival originated our camp-meetings, and in both these denominations they were held every year, and, indeed, have been ever since, more or less. They would erect their camps with logs or frame them, and cover them with clapboards or shingles. They would also erect a shed, sufficiently large to protect five thousand people from wind and rain, and cover it with boards or shingles; build a large stand, seat the shed, and here they would collect together from forty to fifty miles around, sometimes further than that. Ten, twenty, and sometimes thirty ministers, of different denominations, would come together and preach night and day, four or five days together; and, indeed, I have known these camp-meetings to last three or four weeks, and great good resulted from them. I have seen more than a hundred sinners fall like dead men under one powerful sermon, and I have seen and heard more than five hundred Christians all shouting aloud the high praises of God at once; and I will venture to assert that many happy thousands were awakened and converted to God at these camp-meetings. Some sinners mocked, some of the old dry professors opposed, some of the old starched Presbyterian preachers preached against these exercises, but still the work went on and spread almost in every direction, gathering additional force, until our country seemed all coming home to God.

In this great revival the Methodists kept moderately balanced; for we had excellent preachers to steer the ship or guide the flock. But some of our members ran wild, and indulged in some extravagancies that were hard to control.

The Presbyterian preachers and members, not being accustomed to much noise or shouting, when they yielded to it went into great extremes and downright wilderness, to the great injury of the cause of God. Their old preachers licensed a great many young men to preach, contrary to their Confession of Faith. That Confession of Faith required their ministers to believe in unconditional election and reprobation, and the unconditional and final perseverance of the saints. But in this revival they, almost to a man, gave up these points of high Calvinism, and preached a free salvation to all mankind. The Westminister Confession required every man, before he could be licensed to preach, to have a liberal education; but this qualification was dispensed with, and a great many fine men were licensed to preach without this literary qualification or subscribing to those high-toned doctrines of Calvinism.

This state of things produced great dissatisfaction in the Synod of Kentucky, and messenger after messenger was sent to wait on the Presbytery to get them to desist from their erratic course, but without success. Finally they were cited to trial before the constituted authorities of the Church. Some were censured, some were suspended, some retraced their steps, while others surrendered their credentials of ordination, and the rest were cut off from the Church.

While in this amputated condition, they called a general meeting of all their licentiates. They met our presiding elder, J. Page, and a number of Methodist ministers at a quarterly meeting in Logan County, and proposed to join the Methodist Episcopal Church as a body; but our aged ministers declined this offer, and persuaded them to rise up and embody themselves together, and constitute a Church. They reluctantly yielded to this advice, and, in due time and form, constituted what they denominated the "Cumberland Presbyterian Church," and in their confession of faith split, as they supposed, the difference between the Predestinarians and the Methodists, rejecting a partial atonement or special election and reprobation, but retaining the doctrine of the final unconditional perseverance of the saints.

What an absurdity! While a man remains a sinner he may come, as a free agent, to Christ, if he will, and if he does not come his damnation will be just, because he refused offered mercy; but as soon as he gets converted his free agency is destroyed, the best boon of Heaven is then lost, and although he may backslide, wander away from Christ, yet he *shall* be brought in. He cannot finally be lost if he has ever been really converted to God.

They make a very sorry show in their attempt to support this left foot of Calvinism. But be it spoken to their credit, they do not often preach this doctrine. They generally preach Methodist doctrine, and have been the means of doing a great deal of good, and would have done much more if they had left this relic of John Calvin behind.

In this revival, usually termed in the West the Cumberland revival, many joined the different Churches, especially the Methodist and Cumberland Presbyterians. The Baptists also came in for a share of the converts, but not to any great extent. Infidelity quailed before the mighty power of God, which was displayed among the people. Universalism was almost driven from the land. The Predestinarians of almost all sorts put forth a mighty effort to stop the work of God.

Just in the midst of our controversies on the subject of the powerful exercises among the people under preaching, a new exercise broke out among us, called the *jerks,* which was overwhelming in its effects upon the bodies and minds of the people. No matter whether they were saints or sinners, they would be taken under a warm song or sermon, and seized with a convulsive jerking all over, which they could not by any possibility avoid, and the more they resisted the more they jerked. If they would not strive against it and pray in good earnest, the jerking would usually abate. I have seen more than five hundred persons jerking at one time in my large congregations. Most usually persons taken with the jerks, to obtain relief, as they said, would rise up and dance. Some would run, but could not get away. Some would resist; on such the jerks were generally very severe.

To see those proud young gentlemen and young ladies, dressed in their silks, jewelry, and prunella, from top to toe, take the *jerks,* would often excite my risibilities. The first jerk or so, you would see their fine bonnets, caps, and combs fly; and so sudden would be the jerking of the head that their long loose hair would crack almost as loud as a wagoner's whip.

At one of my appointments in 1804 there was a very large congregation turned out to hear the Kentucky boy, as they called me. Among the rest there were two very finely-dressed, fashionable young ladies, attended by two brothers with loaded horsewhips. Although the house was large; it was crowded. The two young ladies, coming in late, took their seats near where I stood, and their two brothers stood in the door. I was a little unwell, and I had a phial of peppermint in my pocket. Before I commenced preaching I took out my phial and swallowed a little of the peppermint. While I was preaching, the congregation was melted into tears. The two young gentlemen moved off to the yard fence, and both the young ladies took the jerks, and they were greatly mortified about it. There was a great stir in the congregation. Some wept, some shouted, and before our meeting closed several were converted.

As I dismissed the assembly a man stepped up to me, and warned me to be on my guard, for he had heard the two brothers swear they would horsewhip me when meeting was out, for giving their sisters the jerks. "Well," said I, "I'll see to that."

I went out and said to the young men that I understood they intended to horsewhip me for giving their sisters the jerks. One replied that he did. I undertook to expostulate with him on the absurdity of the charge against me, but he swore I need not deny it; for he had seen me take out a phial, in which I carried some truck that gave his sisters the jerks. As quick as thought it came into my mind how I would get clear of my whipping, and, jerking out the peppermint phial, said I "Yes; if I give your sisters the jerks I'll give them to you." In a moment I saw he was scared. I moved toward him, he backed, I advanced, and he wheeled and ran, warning me not to come near him, or he would kill me. It raised the laugh on him, and I escaped my whipping. I had the pleasure, before the year was out, of seeing all four soundly converted to God, and I took them into the Church.

While I am on this subject I will relate a very serious circumstance which I knew to take place with a man who had the jerks at a camp-meeting, on what was called the Ridge, in William Magee's congregation. There was a great work of religion in the encampment. The jerks were very prevalent. There was a company of drunken rowdies who came to interrupt the meeting. These rowdies were headed by a very large drinking man. They came with their bottles of whiskey in their pockets. This large man cursed the jerks, and all religion. Shortly afterward he took the jerks, and he started to run, but he jerked so powerfully he could not get away. He halted among some saplings, and, although he was violently agitated, he took out his bottle of whiskey, and swore he would drink the damned jerks to death; but he jerked at such a rate he could not get the bottle to his mouth, though he tried hard. At length he fetched a sudden jerk, and the bottle struck a sapling and was broken to pieces, and spilled his whiskey on the ground. There was a great crowd gathered round him, and when he lost his whiskey he became very much enraged, and cursed and swore very profanely, his jerks still increasing. At length he fetched a very violent jerk, snapped his neck, fell, and soon expired, with his mouth full of cursing and bitterness.

I always looked upon the jerks as a judgment sent from God, first, to bring sinners to repentance; and, secondly, to show professors that God could work with or without means, and that he could work over and above means, and do whatsoever seemeth him good, to the glory of his grace and the salvation of the world.

There is no doubt in my mind that, with weak-minded, ignorant, and superstitious persons, there was a great deal of sympathetic feeling with many that claimed to be under the influence of this jerking exercise; and yet, with many, it was perfectly involuntary. It was, on all occasions, my practice to recommend fervent prayer as a remedy, and it almost universally proved an effectual antidote.

There were many other strange and wild exercises into which the subjects of this revival fell; such, for instance, as what was called the running, jumping, barking exercise. The Methodist preachers generally preached against this extravagant wildness. I did it uniformly in my little ministrations, and sometimes gave great offense; but I feared no consequences when I felt my awful responsibilities to God. From these wild exercises, another great evil arose from the heated and wild imaginations of some. They professed to fall into trances and see visions; they would fall at meetings and sometimes at home, and lay apparently powerless and motionless for days, sometimes for a week at a time, without food or drink; and when they came to, they professed to have seen heaven and hell, to have seen God, angels, the devil and the damned; they would prophesy, and, under the pretense of Divine inspiration, predict the time of the end of the world, and the ushering in of the great millennium.

This was the most troublesome delusion of all; it made such an appeal to the ignorance, superstition, and credulity of the people, even saint as well as sinner. I watched this matter with a vigilant eye. If I opposed it, I would have to meet the clamor of the multitude; and if any one opposed it, these very visionists would single him out, and denounce the dreadful judgments of God against him. They would even set the very day that God was to burn the world, like the self-deceived modern Millerites. They would prophesy, that if any one did oppose them, God would send fire down from heaven and consume him, like the blasphemous Shakers. They would proclaim that they could heal all manner of diseases, and raise the dead, just like the diabolical Mormons. They professed to have converse with spirits of the dead in heaven and hell, like the modern spirit rappers. Such a state of things I never saw before, and I hope in God I shall never see again.

I pondered well the whole matter in view of my responsibilities, searched the Bible for the true fulfillment of promise and prophecy, prayed to God for light and Divine aid, and proclaimed open war against these delusions. In the midst of them along came the Shakers, and Mr. Rankin, one of the Presbyterian revival preachers, joined them; Mr. G. Wall, a visionary local preacher among the Methodists, joined them; all the country was in commotion.

I made public appointments and drew multitudes together, and openly showed from the Scriptures that these delusions were false. Some of these visionary men and women prophesied that God would kill me. The Shakers soon pretended to seal my damnation. But nothing daunted, for I knew Him in whom I had believed, I threw my appointments in the midst of them, and proclaimed to listening thousands the more sure word of prophecy. This mode of attack threw a damper on these visionary, self-deluded, false prophets, sobered some, reclaimed others, and stayed the fearful tide of delusion that was sweeping over the country.

I will here state a case which occurred at an early day in the State of Indiana, in a settlement called Busroe. Many of the early emigrants to that settlement were Methodists, Baptists, and Cumberland Presbyterians. The Shaker priests, all apostates from the Baptist and the Cumberland Presbyterians, went over among them. Many of them I was personally acquainted with, and had given them letters when they moved from Kentucky to that new country. There were then no Methodist circuit preachers in that region.

There was an old Brother Collins, a local preacher, who withstood these Shakers, and in private combat he was a full match for any of them, but he was not eloquent in public debate, and hence the Shaker priests overcame my old brother, and by scores swept members of different Churches away from their steadfastness into the muddy pool of Shakerism.

The few who remained steadfast sent to Kentucky for me, praying me to come and help them. I sent an appointment, with an invitation to meet any or all of the Shaker priests in public debate; but instead of meeting me, they appointed a meeting in opposition, and warned the believers, as they called them, to keep away from my meeting; but from our former acquaintance and intimate friendship, many of them came to hear me. I preached to a vast crowd for about three hours, and I verily believe God helped me. The very foundations of every Shaker present were shaken from under him. They then besought me to go to the Shaker meeting that night. I went, and when I got there we had a great crowd. I proposed to them to have a debate, and they dared not refuse. The terms were these: A local preacher I had with me was to ôpen the debate; then one or all of their preachers, if they chose, were to follow, and I was to bring up the rear. My preacher opened the debate by merely stating the points of difference. Mr. Brayelton followed, and, instead of argument, he turned everything into abuse and insulting slander. Then he closed, and Mr. Gill rose, but, instead of argument, he uttered a few words of personal abuse, and then called on all the Shakers to meet him a few minutes in the yard, talk a little, and then disperse.

Our debate was out in the open air, at the end of a cabin. I rose, called them to order, and stated that it was fairly agreed by these Shaker priests that I should bring up the rear, or close the argument. I stated that it was cowardly to run; that if I was the devil himself, and they were right, I could not hurt them. I got the most of them to take their seats and hear me. Mr. Gill gathered a little band, and he and they left. They had told the people in the day that if I continued to oppose them, God would make an example of me, and send fire from heaven and consume me. When I rose to reply I felt a Divine sense of the approbation of God, and that he would give me success.

I addressed the multitude about three hours, and when I closed my argument I opened the door of the Church, and invited all that would renounce Shakerism to come and give me their hand. Forty-seven came forward, and then and there openly renounced the dreadful delusion. The next day I followed those that fled; and the next day I went from cabin to cabin, taking the names of those that returned to the solid foundation of truth, and my number rose to eighty-seven. I then organized them into a regular society, and the next fall had a preacher sent to them. And perhaps this victory may be considered among the first-fruits of Methodism in that part of this new country. This was in 1808. . . .

In the course of this year, 1834, we had a camp-meeting in Knox County, Illinois, Henderson River Mission. There was a goodly number tented, and a fine turnout of people, for the number of settlers in this new and rising country. Our encampment was pitched in a beautiful little grove, on an eminence, surrounded by prairie on every hand.

There was in this settlement an interesting and intelligent family from one of the Eastern states. The younger members of the family consisted of several young men and young ladies. The young people liked the Methodists, and were deeply convicted; the old people, particularly the old lady, were very much opposed to them. Living, as they did, close by the camp ground, they put their Yankee ingenuity to work to keep their children away from the meeting; but finding they could not accomplish it, they at once determined to pitch their tent on the camp ground, and then they thought they would have a better opportunity to watch the children, and counteract any influence we might exert upon them. They pretended to be very friendly, to save appearances. The old lady, for the purpose of disarming me, treated me very kindly, and invited me to eat with them, which I did. In the meantime one of the daughters, who was deeply convicted, told me all about her mother's opposition to the Methodists, and her schemes to prevent her children from being influenced to become religious.

One Saturday evening I invited the seekers of religion to come forward to the altar for the prayers of the Church. Two of her daughters came forward and knelt in prayer. A younger sister, almost as much opposed to the Methodists as her mother, went into the altar with a vial of hartshorn, and while her two sisters were trying to pray she slipped the hartshorn to their nose, in order to drive them up and prevent their seeking religion. I very soon detected her in her operations, and took hold of her hand, wrenched the vial from her, led her out of the altar, and told her if I caught her in there any more on such business, I would pitch her out and publicly expose her.

While I was talking to and praying with these two young ladies, and others, I saw the old lady, their mother, come and take her seat outside of the altar, immediately opposite her daughters, and if at any time she thought I was not watching her, she would kick them in their sides to drive them up. I watched her very closely, and when in the act of kicking them, I took hold of her foot and gave her a strong push backward, and over she tumbled among the benches. Being a large corpulent woman, she had some considerable tussel to right herself again. So in this way I defeated the scheme of the devil once more. The girls became very much engaged, but while there were many still pressing to the altar, and my attention for a moment was called off, the old lady contrived to get them out of the altar into the tent. As soon as I discovered what was done, I gathered two or three good singers and praying persons, and followed them into the tent, and commenced singing; I then gave them an exhortation; then said, "Let us pray," and called on the father of the girls to pray for his children, but he refused; I then called on their mother to kneel down and pray for her children, and she refused. In the meantime two of the boys, as well as the two girls, became very much affected, and cried for mercy; and presently the third daughter, that had used the hartshorn in the altar, got awfully convicted, and begged all present to pray for her, as she would be lost and damned forever. This was too much for the old people; they became awfully alarmed, and wept bitterly; and you may be sure the whole tent was in a mightly uproar. The singing, praying, and exhortations were kept up nearly all night.

Four of the family were powerfully converted, and the sectarian devil in the old father amd mother was effectually disarmed, and from that blessed night they became a religious family; all joined the Methodist Church, and, as far as I know, walked worthy of their high vocation. May they all prove faithful till death, and then receive a crown of life.

While on the Quincy District—the town of Quincy was a very small and sickly place—I remember spending near two weeks in it when, if my recollection serves me, there was but one family where there was no affliction. In some families there were one, two, or three confined to their beds with fever, and sometimes the whole family were sick together, and not one able to help another. I went from house to house, not only to minister to their temporal wants, but to pray with them, and point the sick and dying to Christ. Many died, and it was with great difficulty that we could muster enough persons able to bury the dead.

There was one case which, in a very special manner, affected my mind. Under the hill, close by the brink of the river, there was what was called a tavern. It was a poor, filthy place at best; the general resort of boatmen, and, in a word, all kinds of bad company resorted to this house. A young man, from some of the eastern states, had come out to explore the west, and was taken sick on the boat, on the river, and was left at this miserable house. He was a professed Christian, and a member of the Methodist Church. No medical aid could be obtained, no nurse, and, in a word, no care was taken of him. In this deplorable condition, he heard that there was a Methodist preacher in town, visiting the sick. He sent for me, and I went to see him. He told me who he was, where his parents lived, and that he had a considerable sum of money with him, and he wanted me to take charge of it, for he was sure if it was known he had money, he should be robbed of it. I took charge of his money, told the landlord to give him all the attention he could, and I would see him paid. The sick man said he was sensible he must die, but that he was not willing to die at that house, and begged me to have him removed, if possible. I knew of a very comfortable place, a few miles in the country, and caused his removal there. Here he lingered for a while, and then died. He had requested me, in case of his decease, to have him decently buried, pay out of his money his tavern bill, his funeral expenses, and write to his parents, that they might come to get his clothes and money. I did as requested. His younger brother came, got his money and clothes, and although it was a mournful dispensation to his relatives, yet it afforded them great comfort to know that he died among friends, though strangers.

This is one among many cases of the kind that from an early day came under my notice, in which enterprising men have come to the far West, have been taken sick, and died among strangers, uncared for.

We had a camp-meeting in Adams County, Quincy Circuit, and it was numerously attended. There was a gracious work of religion going on among the people, and there was a pretty clever, intelligent old gentleman, who had moved into the settlement from Kentucky, who, in that State, had been a Baptist preacher, but had got his mind confused with Alexander Campbell's dogmas about experimental religion. He had a fine family, and some of them knew what real religion was. He and family attended our camp-meeting. He was very fond of argument on almost all theological subjects. He tried to get me into debate during the meeting, but I told him I was there for other and better business. He denied the operations of the Spirit, its testimony, bearing witness with our spirits; that we are the children of God, and that all those happy feelings professed by Christians were nothing but excitement; that there was no religion in it.

On Sunday night a most tremendous power fell on the assembly, and a general shout went up to heaven from hundreds of Christians. Among the crowd of happy and shouting Christians this gentleman's wife and daughter were exceedingly happy, and shouted aloud. The old gentleman could not stand it; he fled behind the tent, lighted his pipe, and tried to smoke away his bad feelings. After laboring in the altar a long time, I stepped back to get a drink of water, and there sat this old Campbellite preacher, and the cloud of smoke from his pipe was fearful; he seemed to be insensible of what he was about, and the pipe and tobacco were paying tribute to his reveries at a mighty rate. I stepped up to him and tapped him on the shoulder, and said, "Come, Mr.——, go with me, and I will show you more happy Christians than you ever saw among the Campbellites in all your life."

"Sir," said he, "it is all delusion; they are not happy."

"But," said I, "your wife and daughter are among the foremost shouters in the crowd. Come," said I, "you must come with me to the altar; I want to pray for you there, that you may get religion, and be happy too. Come, sir, I want to see you converted, and shouting-happy." I took him by the arm, to lead him to the altar, but he drew back. I gathered him again, and pulled him along; but the moment he saw his wife and daughter shouting, and making toward him, he tore loose from my grasp, and actually ran. Poor man, he was so confused by fishing in the muddy waters of Campbellism, that he lost his mental balance. He would not yield to the Spirit of God, and submit to be an humble, shouting, happy Christian. Sometimes he would talk rational; sometimes quote, and apply the Scriptures right; then, again, he became skeptical. But the great difficulty was, the pride of his professed ministerial standing would not let him yield, and renounce his errors. Thus he worried on for a considerable time, and was carried into the whirlpool of doubt and unbelief. His friends talked to him, but talked in vain. He became more and more flighty in his mind, till at length, in a paroxysm of insanity, he shot himself. This event fell like a thunderbolt on his family and the surrounding community; and proves that it is a hard thing to fight against God.

VII. DEATH

Death is always harder on the living than on the dead. On the frontier, where the population was small, where friends and relatives were far away, this was particularly true. Whose deaths were felt the hardest—those of a husband, wife, or child? To whom could survivors turn after the death of a loved one? Was death closer on the frontier than in the settled regions? Did the pioneers have a different attitude about death from people in the settled regions?

Nannie Alderson

To be suddenly left a widow sometimes brought a woman to a discovery of strength and talent she did not know she possessed. (N. T. Alderson and H. H. Hunt, A Bride Goes West, *256-67.)*

There were other signs, there toward the last, to make us feel that our luck was about to change. Friends were pulling hard for us, and the time came, as it is bound to do, when one of them was in a position to make his wishes effective. In 1894 our old partner, Mr. Zook, was elected county assessor, and he made Mr. Alderson his deputy. It was a fine position, and we felt now that everything would be all right.

And so it would have been, beyond a doubt in the world—if the dreadful and unlooked-for had not happened. There is no help in brooding over the evils dealt by fate, or in wondering why this or that was as it was. But it has always been a strange and bitter thought to me, that the anxieties about Mr. Alderson's safety, which haunted me so on the ranch, should have quieted when we came to Miles City. The presence of so many people around seemed to give me a feeling of security, and so, on the afternoon of the accident to my husband, I was happily busy, and had no premonition at all of the greatest tragedy that can come to a wife and mother.

But I must go back a week or more before it happened.

Coming home one afternoon, Mr. Alderson had said cheerily: "What do you think I bought today?"

My heart sank. I answered: "Not another beaded pincushion, I hope!"

The beaded pincushion was a family by-word. For, another time some years before, when we were just as hard up as we were now—and I needing curtains the worst way—Mr. Alderson had seen an old squaw offering this awful-looking thing for sale. She wanted five dollars for it, and looked so disappointed when nobody would buy, that he offered her a dollar—which she snatched at, you may be sure. So home he came with the beaded pincushion.

Now, as before, we were buying only what we absolutely needed and we had to do without a great deal of that. So no wonder I was dismayed when Mr. Alderson said: "What do you think I bought today?"

He went on to tell me that on his way home he had passed the sale corrals on Main Street, where Judge Brown, the livery stable keeper and a great friend of his, was holding an auction. To explain how a livery stable man came to hold the title of "Judge," I need only say that Judge Brown once had held office as justice of the peace. Mr. Alderson climbed up on the fence along with others to watch the sale, when Judge Brown turned to him and said: "Just look at this, Walt. Here is a four-year-old, not a blemish on him, gentle, and I'm only offered five dollars for him."

Mr. Alderson said: "Why, I'd give you seven."

It was the highest bid—and he came home leading the horse, which we named Seven Dollars.

The fact that we had any quantity of horses on the range, and good ones too, which we couldn't sell but on which we had to pay taxes, put this "buy" in the class with the beaded pincushion—no doubt about it.

But my husband, who was always optimistic, said: "I'll get my money out of Seven Dollars, for he's well broken, and I need a horse right now to drive with that filly, whose mate I had to shoot.''

The loss of this filly had been one of many discouragements. She had slipped on the ice and broken her leg, but my husband had set her leg and put her in a swing, hoping to save her for breeding purposes. She was doing well when the swing slipped, and she was so badly hurt that she had to be put out of the way.

Since his appointment as deputy assessor Mr. Alderson knew that he should have many miles of traveling to do, not all of it on horseback and for this reason he wanted to break in Seven Dollars as the other member of his team. On the day of the accident, he left early in the morning, driving the new horse and the surviving filly, and he asked me to come and open the gate leading out of the stable yard. I opened the gate, and the two horses started off as if they had always been driven together. When Mr. Alderson returned several hours later it was beginning to storm, and he called to me not to come out to open the gate, as the horses were gentle and would stand. The last time I saw him conscious, was when he got out of the light driving cart, holding the reins in his hand, opened the gate and went on into the stable.

With the unending optimism of ranchmen about horses, a friend of ours had just brought in a gaited stallion from Missouri, preparatory to breeding still more saddle animals for a five-dollar market. My husband had insisted upon his keeping the new horse in our stable, until he was rested sufficiently from his train trip to be taken out to the ranch. The stallion had been very restless and had been kicking and whinnying whenever anyone entered the barn. But I had thought nothing of it.

When Mr. Alderson didn't come to the house right away I thought that with his usual kindness to dumb animals, he was making them comfortable, even to currying them free of the slushy ice from the drive. So I went about my work while the two younger children were playing, and the older ones not yet home from school.

The first intimation I had of anything like a tragedy was when the living room door opened and our Doctor looked in, closing the door before I could speak to him. Opening the door again, I saw the Doctor and Sheriff Hawkins disappear around the house, saw them vault over the fence without waiting to open the gate. As I hurried to the back porch, another friend was coming to meet me, both hands reaching out in tender friendliness.

"Walt has been badly hurt," he said, "we think kicked in the head. You must be brave and help me."

I thought if he was kicked in the head the two babies must not see their father so, and I picked them up and ran across the street to a good neighbor, telling her the little I knew and asking that she keep them till I could come again for them. Then I helped Mr. Hastings get the bed ready. Then doctors and friends carried my husband in.

He had been found lying face downward on the stable floor, with the imprint of two horse's hoofs on his head. From the position of the horses when they found him, they argued that he must have let Seven Dollars go to his stall, while he was tying the filly; that Seven Dollars, being loose, had backed out and started kicking at the stallion, and as the fight broke out with that lightning-like fury, to which I had once been witness, Mr. Alderson was somehow caught between them.

They gave me no hope from the first, but as the days and nights passed and he became apparently more comfortable, I did hope in spite of all they said. All that our two good doctors and the surgeon from Fort Keogh could do was done, but the fracture extended to the base of the brain, and he was never himself again. He died after six days, on the 18th of March, 1895.

People were so kind, so incredibly kind; and one of the most faithful was our dear friend, Judge Brown, the auctioneer. He was at my husband's bedside from morning till night, it seemed, to the neglect of his business; there were still no nurses in Miles City, and strange as it may seem the doctors turned to the big, uncouth-looking livery-stable keeper, rather than to some woman, when my husband had to be moved or an operation attempted.

Because it was winter and there was no active work on the range, the stockmen were all in Miles City, and they were in our house constantly. The second night after the accident, I saw a group of them talking in the dining room. Among them was a man whose family was keeping the older children, and who was also our life insurance agent.

He came to me and asked: "Do you know where Mr. Alderson's insurance papers are?"

I went to the desk and found the papers, and gave them to him. I saw him, back in the next room, unfold the papers while a crowd of men looked on, read through them, and heard one voice after another say: "Thank God."

He told me later that man after man had come to him with money, offering to fix up the insurance policy in case my husband had not kept it paid up—if it were not too late to fix it. When the seventh man came at midnight with money, he came to ask me for the papers!

The years since then have been close-packed and strenuous as before. But after my husband's death, I was no longer a bride who went west, nor a woman who was helping to open up a new country; I was merely an overworked mother of four, trying to make ends meet under conditions which were none too easy. For seven years after Mr. Alderson's death we lived in Miles City, where I did what I could to support the children and myself. I ran a boarding house; I made bread and sold it; I kept a cow and sold the milk; I had a little catering business. I never had any help except now and then a man to milk the cow, and once in awhile an old darky woman—just about the only one in town—who lent a hand when I was getting up a supper for the Masons on Lodge nights. Mr. Alderson had been a Mason, and they were faithful customers. I always liked catering for men. They were always generous, and they never fussed about little things.

Anne Ellis

The loss of loved ones brought others to the edge of despair. (A. Ellis, The Life of an Ordinary Woman, *202-07, 262-69.)*

George has rented a little three-room house. It is luxury for me to have a bedroom; we have plenty to eat and pass a very peaceful, contented month. But soon George starts to complain that it was run by a bunch of 'red necks,' 'chaws,' 'flannel mouths,' 'Micks'—all names for Irishmen. At this time there was an agitation against Catholics by an organization of men called the American Protective Association, to which George belonged. (All my life I have had the utmost respect and toleration for any and all religions, and envied people who were brought up in any faith, whether Catholic or Jew.) All this fuss worried me and at last it reached such a state that George was either fired or quit.

He then got a job on the Vindicator at Independence. All these towns are in what is called the Cripple Creek district, the largest being Cripple Creek, then Victor (where we lived), four or five miles from Cripple Creek; Independence is halfway up the mountain-side, on top is Altman, at the foot Goldfield. Soon we move to another house and I help load, the expressman showing me how to take hold of a trunk so that it will load easy. Again the babies and I climb in with him and are off. This house was a two-room frame, built in the mountain-side. To get in the front room, one had to climb a flight of twelve or fifteen rickety steps, while the back door was even with the ground. It was newly papered, and I at once put newspapers back of the dry-goods box we washed on, and the table where we ate, thereby winning the friendship of the landlady, a German woman, supposed to be the hardest-boiled in the district. She owned the row where the fast girls had their cribs, and had the Indian sign on them, as she could and would fight any or all of them. Between-times she drove a burro cart to back doors collecting slop, but I found later that when I needed a friend she stood by. In the front room there was a bed, a stand, and always the same shelf in the corner to hang clothes under. On the floor was my first carpet, a bright red velvet one, over which I was much set up. I imagine she bought it for one of the cribs, then changed her mind. The house joined a livery stable, but I tried to think the smell coming through the wall was healthy, and got so the pawing and stamping of the horses was company to me.

If one would let one's self, one could be very lonesome, not knowing anybody, and with one's husband gone all day. Oh, it was a dull life! You see, there were no cheap amusements in those days, no picture shows; the kind of people I would have cared to meet I had no chance of meeting, and had I met them they would not have cared for me. I suppose I could have gone to church and met people, but I was too honorable to use the church as an excuse to 'get in,' when I felt no urge to go from a religious standpoint.

One cold night I was awakened by a strange dream, a veil-like presence trying to give me a message. I was not at all frightened, and got up to put more cover on Neita, who was sleeping in her little home-made bed. I returned shivering to my own bed and cuddled Joy to keep her warm (she is six months old now); these little framehouses were so cold everything would freeze solid. Then I listened for a time to the horses pawing and stamping, then was asleep again, leaving a candle burning, and was again awakened by this strange dream. Now I lay there, neither asleep nor awake, wondering if there were anything in dreams, and, if so, what did mine mean?

Soon I hear voices in the front yard. At once I jump from bed, not stopping to dress, rush and open the front door, look down the flight of steps at the figures standing there, and ask, 'Why don't you bring him on in?'

Some of the men climb these rickety steps, take hold of me, and ask, 'Is this where George Fleming lives?'

'Yes, why don't you bring him in? Is he hurt bad?'

Now he calls down, 'This is the place, boys'—and to me, 'You must get some clothes on, it is very cold.'

I throw a quilt around me, and they come in, several of them, but they are bearing no burden. All carefully remove their hats as they enter the door. They fill this small room. One starts a fire. Neita is wakened by the noise and sits up in bed; Joy begins to cry and I go to her.

A man says, 'That's a fine boy you got there.'

Again I ask, 'Where is George?'

Only now do they answer, one for all, each looking helpless. 'Well, you see, he is hurt—'

I break in, 'Yes, I know. Bad?'

'Well, Mam, you see he drilled into a missed hole, and here we didn't know he had a family. It is shore bad, and anything we can do only mention it, and—yes, Mam, he is bad.'

'Well, then, we will go to him.'

'But—well, Mam, you might as well know. He is dead, shot all to pieces.'

I just melt on the floor, the quilt covering me. One of the men says, 'Look, boys, and see if there is any whiskey or camfire,' and tries to raise me, but I, dry-eyed and voiced, ask them to leave me alone for a while.

They all troop through the kitchen and out the back door, except two, who sit there till morning with me, bolt upright in their chairs, only relaxing to hold the children. I still crouch there, gritting my teeth and clenching my hands. As it is coming daylight, Joy cries so hard that I know she is hungry and get up to let her nurse, but—there is no milk now, and never is again. After this night she has to be fed till I get a bottle for her. Strange, what a shock will do.

Now I dress and prepare breakfast for us all. These everyday duties are the saving of one in trouble. After eating, the men leave me; I am alone and glad of it. I go in the yard and a spirit of rebellion at fate comes over me. It is all centered around the fact that my children will be as I was, never a father to care for or look out for them. Most of my sorrow was for these fatherless children.

Then comes the landlady, very rough and swearing, still kind and gentle. Later in the day, some Knights of Pythias come, making all arrangements; then a lawyer from the mine with a paper for me to sign, but I know enough not to. In these times there was no Compensation Fund. I do sign this paper later, releasing the mine from any fault in the matter, and they give me six hundred dollars; in addition to this, each man working in the mine gives me a day's wages. This I take with a feeling of shame, because I know what a day's pay means to some of their families. Some of the miners' wives come, but how can they comfort this silent, dry-eyed creature who doesn't act like any other woman would, and it is as hard on them to make conversation as it is for me to answer. I am glad when they leave. That evening after dark comes a tap on the door, and a big Irishwoman comes in—under her arm a small bundle of dark outing flannel which she hands me. 'Here, dear, make a petticoat for the wee wan. Me man was kilt, too, about wan month gone. Oh, the throuble, the throuble'—and she begins to cry. I, too, at this, open up and we cry together, for ourselves, for each other, and for all sorrowing womankind. After this I feel better and go to sleep, making plans for the future. Henry comes for the funeral; also the cousin from Denver, the Crails from Gunnison, and George's mother from Saguache.

The cousin takes charge of everything; the rest are helpless. I have a long veil, the miners send a big bunch of carnations—and I insist on carrying them! My only excuse is I never had any boughten flowers before, and that I love them so. I carry them much as one would a graduation bouquet, and have a feeling of importance as I step in the carriage.

George has been taken to the undertaker—the usual way now, but unheard of then. When we see him at the cemetery, he is only a form dressed in his clothes, with face and hands all wrapped in white bandages. Afterward in day-dreams, I imagined it was not he at all, and that he had left and gone to Alaska, from where he would return wealthy and shower gifts on the children and me.

After we are home again, this question comes up, What am I going to do? I don't know, except not give up the children. The cousin suggests I go and take a business course, but I will not hear of any one having the children, even for that long. I can see now how foolish this was, as in the long run it would have been better for all of us; but this was another move where I blindly changed our lives in a twinkling. Rosie and George's mother think I will manage somehow. I am glad and lonesome when they are gone. The first thing I do is to order a tombstone, no doubt foolish, but I feel he gave his life for these few hundred dollars I have, and that this is the least I can do.

Not long afterward, Anne accepted a proposal of marriage from another miner and they moved to another mining town nearby.

During this time Joy gets a sore throat. I have always been my own doctor, so now do all the things I have formerly done. While she does not seem bad, playing each day, she gets no better, and still I do not pay much attention to her. She and Neita are sleeping in an old tent beside the house, and on the third day, when she comes in covered with blood, I see there is more the matter than I can reach with my Listerine, tincture of iron, and Wizard Oil. (How I hated to spend the money even for these!) I send for the doctor, who pronounces it diphtheria (that dread word!) and gives both her and Neita antitoxin. I hate it—although it may save lives, it leaves many cripples, or did then. I doctor Joy every half-hour day and night, and she seems to be improving and I am so glad to see her strong. The doctor did not caution me in regard to her heart being weak. Diphtheria is such a loathsome disease, with such an odor, and, you see, we were cooking, eating, and sleeping all in this one room. It was summer and very hot. Each day, I would wash and mop, and I kept a wet blanket hanging from the ceiling in a draft, trying to keep things cool. (When you reach a certain stage, you do not think of expense.)

Comes a day when she is very much better. We are invited to a Masonic dance, and I am very anxious to go, as this will be the first time I have gone to a social gathering in Goldfield. I know I cannot go, yet put my hair up in curlers. I have made Joy some paper dolls to play with while lying there. Everything is very quiet. I am sitting on the trunk reading 'The Count of Monte Cristo,' and when she asks me for a drink I never look up (oh, the bitterness of it!) but say, 'Neita, give Joy a drink.' Neita is reading also, and doesn't move. There come a gurgle from the bed, 'I want a drink.' How I throw the book behind the trunk (and shudder at the name even now) and jump for the bed, but it is too late—Joy turns on her side, and, with a sigh, is gone. I scream at Neita to run for the doctor, which she does, down the half-mile of hot, dusty road, while I am doing all in my power for Joy, tearing at the curlers with one hand, feeling them burn into my head, to think of being so foolish when she was so bad.

The doctor comes and pulls the sheet up over her face, and now I know this is the end. Some one goes in search of Herbert, who is out looking for work. I do not remember what followed, only that I would not let her be taken to the undertaker's, but did all things for her myself, combing her beautiful hair for the last time, dressing her in her many-times-washed-and let-down white dress. Each thing I do, each move I make, I am choked with bitterness and sorrow, thinking of the many times I have punished her, of the time she must learn 'Old Glory' to speak at an entertainment. She was always so full of play that she put it off to the last minute, then I whipped her, making her climb on the old swelled-top trunk, not letting her come down till she knew it. Of the Fourth of July—when I dress her in the Indian blanket and she wins a prize, but escapes in the crowd, and I frightened, nervous, and scolding, find her in the judges' stand, her brown eyes dancing. And the day she drapes the veil around her and dances on the rock up by the Malapai, I stopping her for fear some one might see her. And what if they had, she was so graceful and pretty!

And thus my thoughts go on and on, filled with sorrow and regret. Night comes and Mrs. S., the woman whom I had sewed with, sends a bunch of flowers, carnations and baby's breath. I have her fixed in the cabin, we go in the tent to sleep, and at once I drop into the deepest sleep I have ever known. Neighbors come to see, and to sympathize with us, and, instead of finding me prostrate and grieving, find me in this deep, peaceful sleep. I think both they and Herbert wondered at me.

The next day, just our family and a minister in one carriage—she in an express wagon—go out the long road to the cemetery, where she is laid between a murdered fast woman and a famous gambler, and, I thought, if she can, she will put in a word for both of them at the big gate. I crouch beside the grave, and when I arise am a better woman than ever before, more human, more lenient toward faults in others, with more feeling and understanding for people, seeing now that money isn't everything, and, from that day to this, while I may have fallen short in some of these things, I never have been as frantic for money as I was before. (It was never the money, only the things I wanted to get with it.)

The first birthday (hers, the tenth, came in a few weeks after she was buried) is the time mothers suffer most. Then, during the holidays, there is more of that aching loss. And it is many, many years before you do not look up, startled—no, not startled, because you expect it, feeling they are with you. Hundreds of times you start to put on their place at the table, or plan for clothes—she will have this; but the keenest of all is when it is stormy, and you think this one is safe here or there, for a moment it flashes in your mind—that she isn't in yet. And now, when I sit resting and thinking of my children's well-being, running over in my mind just where they are and what they will be doing, always at these times I count one boy and two girls.

Before the quarantine is over, Neita comes down with it, but I am on the job this time, and do not let her move head or hands. As I work, I am having a struggle with Fate and myself, although it is a silent one, as I never told Herbert any of my thoughts. First, you see, I had no religion or faith to fall back on. Would I ever see her again? I could not bear the thought that I might not, and I think the thought of this, and the feeling that I must have some one to lean on, brought me to find God—I wonder if we would have much religion without trouble and sorrow? Then there was the fight—what is it all about, anyway? There is no use in trying, we are only born for work and worry, and I wished I was dead and out of it all. I am taking care of a miner's room near by, and when I make the bed, find a gun under the pillow. I often think to-day I will end it, and go so far as to lift the gun (very carefully, as I am afraid of guns, and the darned thing might go off) and stand in front of the mirror seeing just how to place it.

One day, in my ceaseless round of work, just after putting a large washing on the line and scrubbing, I have a miscarriage. If I think at all, I am pleased over this, and never stop working day or night. On the third day I am lifting something and have a dreadful hemorrhage, and I, who so lately wished to die (I have often smiled to myself over this), call some passer-by to get the doctor quick, then go to bed (with Neita), piling pillows under my hips, and lying there scarcely breathing, waiting and praying for help. I have never thought of killing myself since. Fate was slapping me hard, trying to knock some sort of a woman into shape.

The Donner Disaster

In 1846, a party of emigrants to California was trapped by heavy snow in a pass on the crest of the Sierra Nevada. Their fate is one of the most famous episodes of suffering in the history of the frontier, and the question of whether the elements or the Donner party themselves were to blame for the tragedy is still debated. (E. Bryant, What I Saw in California *(1848), 225-30, 232-37.)*

Copy of a Journal kept by a suffering emigrant on the California mountains, from

Oct. 31st, 1846, to March 1st, 1847

TRUCKEE LAKE, Nov. 20, 1846.—Came to this place on the 31st of last month; went into the Pass, the snow so deep we were unable to find the road, and when within three miles from the summit, turned back to this shanty on Truckee Lake. Stanton came up one day after we arrived here; we again took our teams and wagons and made another unsuccessful attempt to cross in company with Stanton; we returned to the shanty, it continuing to snow all the time. We now have killed most part of our cattle, having to remain here until next spring, and live on lean beef without bread or salt. It snowed during the space of eight days with little intermission, after our arrival here, though now clear and pleasant, freezing at night, the snow nearly gone from the valleys,—21. Fine morning, wind N. W.; twenty-two of our company about starting to cross the mountains this day including Stanton and his Indians.—22. Froze hard last night; fine and clear to-day; no account from those on the mountains.—23. Same weather, wind W.; the expedition across the mountains returned after an unsuccessful attempt.—25. Cloudy, looks like the eve of a snow-storm; our mountaineers are to make another trial to-morrow, if fair;—froze hard last night.—26. Began to snow last evening, now rains or sleets; the party does not start to-day.—29. Still snowing, snow about three feet deep; wind W., killed my last oxen to-day; gave another yoke to Foster; wood hard to be got.—30. Snowing fast, looks as likely to continue as when it commenced; no living thing without wings can get about.

Dec. 1.—Still snowing, wind W.; snow about six or six and a half feet deep; very difficult to get wood, and we are completely housed up; our cattle all killed but two or three, and these, with the horses and Stanton's mules, all supposed to be lost in the snow; no hopes of finding them alive.—3. Ceased snowing; cloudy all day; warm enough to thaw.—5. Beautiful sunshine, thawing a little; looks delightful after the long storm; now seven or eight feet deep.—6. The morning fine and clear; Stanton and Graves manufacturing snow-shoes for another scrabble; no account of mules.—8. Fine weather, froze hard last night; wind S. W.; hard work to find wood sufficient to keep us warm or cook our beef.—9. Commenced snowing about 11 o'clock, wind N. W.; took in Spitzer yesterday so weak, that he cannot rise without help, caused by starvation. Some have a scant supply of beef; Stanton trying to get some for himself and Indians; not likely to get much.—10. Snowed fast all night with heavy squalls of wind; continues to snow, now about seven feet in depth.—13. Snows faster than any previous day; Stanton and Graves, with several others, making preparations to cross the mountains on snow-shoes. Snow eight feet deep on a level.—16. Fair and pleasant, froze hard last night; the company started on snow-shoes to cross the mountains, wind S. E.—17. Pleasant. Wm. Murphy returned from the mountain party last evening; Balis Williams died night before last; Milton and Noah started for Donner's eight days ago; not returned yet; think they are lost in the snow.—19. Snowed last night, thawing to-day, wind N.W.; a little singular for a thaw.—20. Clear and pleasant; Mrs. Reed here; no account from Milton yet; Charles Berger [Burger] set out for Donner's; turned back, unable to proceed; tough times, but not discouraged; our hopes are in God, Amen.—21. Milton got back last night from Donner's camp; sad news, Jacob Donner, Samuel Shoemaker, Rhinehart, [Rinehart] and Smith are dead the rest of them in a low situation; snowed all night with a strong S. W. wind.—23. Clear to-day; Milton took some of his meat away; all well at their camp. Began this day to read the "Thirty day's prayers." Almighty God grant the requests of unworthy sinners!—24. Rained all night and still continues; poor prospect for any kind of comfort, spiritual or temporal.—25. Began to snow yesterday, snowed all night, and snows yet rapidly; extremely difficult to find wood; offered our prayers to God this Christmas morning; the prospect is appalling, but we trust in Him.—27. Cleared off yesterday, continues clear, snow nine feet deep; wood growing scarce; a tree when felled sinks into the snow and hard to be got at.—30. Fine clear morning, froze hard last night; Charles Berger [Burger] died last evening about ten o'clock.—31. Last of the year; may we, with the help of God, spend the coming year better than we have the past, which we propose to do if it is the will of the Almighty to deliver us from our present dreadful situation. Amen. Morning fair but cloudy, wind E. by S.; looks like another snow-storm—snow-storms are dreadful to us; the snow at present very deep.

Jan. 1. 1847.—We pray the God of mercy to deliver us from our present calamity, if it be His holy will. Commenced snowing last night and snows a little yet; provisions getting very scant; dug up a hide from under the snow yesterday—have not commenced on it yet.—3. Fair during the day, freezing at night; Mrs. Reed talks of crossing the mountains with her children.—4. Fine morning, looks like spring; Mrs. Reed and Virginia, Milton Elliot, and Eliza Williams, started a short time ago with the hope of crossing the mountains; left the children here—it was difficult for Mrs. Reed to part with them—6. Eliza came back from the mountains yesterday evening, not able to proceed, the others kept ahead.—8. Very cold this morning; Mrs. Reed and others came back; could not find the way on the other side of the mountains; they have nothing but hides to live on.—10. Began to snow last night, still continues; wind W. N. W.—13. Snowing fast—snow higher than the shanty; it must be 13 feet deep; cannot get wood this morning; it is a dreadful sight for us to look upon.—14. Cleared off yesterday; the sun shining brilliantly renovates our spirits, praises be to the God of heaven.—15. Clear day again, wind N. W.; Mrs. Murphy blind; Lantron [Landrum] not able to get wood, has but one axe between him and Keysburg; [Keseberg] it looks like another storm—expecting some account from Sutter's soon.—17. Eliza Williams came here this morning; Lantron [Landrum] crazy last night; provisions scarce, hides our main subsistence. May the Almighty send us help.—21. Fine morning; John Batise [Juan Bautista] and Mr. Denton came this morning with Eliza; she will not eat hides. Mrs.—sent her back to live or die on them—22. Began to snow after sunrise; likely to continue; wind W.—23. Blew hard and snowed all night, the most severe storm we have experienced this winter; wind W.—26. Cleared up yesterday; to-day fine and pleasant, wind S.; in hopes we are done with snow-storms; those who went to Sutter's not yet returned; provisions getting scant; people growing weak living on small allowance of hides.—27. Commenced snowing yesterday; still continues to-day; Lewis (Sutter's Indian) died three days ago; wood getting scarce; don't have fire enough to cook our hides.—30. Fair and pleasant, wind W. thawing in the sun; John and Edward Breen went to Graves' this morning; the—seized on Mrs.—goods, until they should be paid; they also took the hides which she and her family subsisted upon. She regained two pieces only, the balance they have taken. You may judge from this what our fare is in camp; there is nothing to be had by hunting, yet perhaps there soon will be.—31. The sun does not shine out brilliantly this morning; froze hard last night, wind N. W. Lantron [Landrum] Murphy died last night about one o'clock. Mrs. Reed went to Graves' this morning to look after goods.

February 5.—Snowed hard until two o'clock last night; many uneasy for fear we shall all perish with hunger; we have but a little meat left and only three hides; Mrs. Reed has nothing but one hide and that is on Graves' house; Milton lives there and likely will keep that—Eddy's child died last night.—6. It snowed faster last night **and to-day than it has done this winter before,** still continues without intermission, wind s. w.; Murphy's folks and Keysburg [Keseberg] say they cannot eat hides; I wish we had enough of them. Mrs. Eddy is very weak.—7. Ceased to snow at last, to-day it is quite pleasant. McCutcheon's child died on the second of this month.—8. Fine clear morning, Spitzer died last night, we shall bury him in the snow. Mrs. Eddy died on the night of the seventh.—9. Mrs. Pike's child all but dead. Milton is at Murphy's not able to get out of bed; Keysburg [Keseberg] never gets up, says he is not able. Mrs. Eddy and child were buried to-day, wind s. E.—10. Beautiful morning, thawing in the sun. Milton Elliott died last night at Murphy's shanty. Mrs. Reed went there this morning to see after effects. J. Denton trying to borrow meat for Graves; had none to give; they had nothing but hides. All are entirely out of meat but a little we have. Our hides are nearly all eat up, but with God's help spring will soon smile upon us.—12. Warm, thawing morning.—14. Fine morning, but cold; buried Milton in the snow. John Denton not well.—15. Morning cloudy until nine o'clock, then cleared off warm. Mrs.—refused to give Mrs.—any hides; put Sutter's pack-hides on her shanty and would not let her have them.—16. Commenced to rain last evening and turned to snow during the night and continued until morning; weather changeable, sunshine then light showers of hail and wind at times. We all feel very unwell; the snow is not getting much less at present.—19. Froze hard last night, seven men arrived from California yesterday evening with provisions, but left the greater part on the way; to-day it is clear and warm for this region. Some of the men have gone to Donner's camp; they will start back on Monday.—22. The Californians started this morning, twenty-four in number, some in a very weak state. Mrs. Keysburg [Keseberg] started with them and left Keysburg [Keseberg] here unable to go; buried Pike's child this morning in the snow, it died two days ago.—23. Froze hard last night, to-day pleasant and thawy; has the appearance of spring, all but the deep snow; winds. s. E.; shot a dog today and dressed his flesh.—25. Today Mrs. Murphy says the wolves are about to dig up the dead bodies around her shanty, and the nights are too cold to watch them, but we hear them howl.—26. Hungry times in camp; plenty of hides, but the folks will not eat them; we eat them with tolerable good appetite, thanks be to the Almighty God. Mrs. Murphy said here yesterday that she thought she would commence on Milton and eat him; I do not think she has done so yet—it is distressing; the Donner's told the California folks four days ago that they would commence on the dead people if they did not succeed that day or next in finding their cattle, then ten or twelve feet under the snow, and did not know the spot or near it; they have done it ere this.—28. One solitary Indian passed by yesterday, came from the Lake, had a heavy pack on his back, gave me five or six roots resembling onions in shape, tasted some like a sweet potato full of tough little fibres.

March 1. Ten men arrived this morning from Bear Valley with provisions; we are to start in two or three days and shall cache our goods here. They say the snow will remain until June.

*

The above mentioned ten men started for the valley with seventeen of the suffers; they travelled fifteen miles and a severe snow-storm came on; they left fourteen of the emigrants, the writer of the above journal and his family, and succeded in getting in but three children. Lieut. Woodworth immediately went to their assistance, but before he reached them they had eaten three of their number, who had died from hunger and fatigue; the remainder Lieut. Woodworth's party brought in. On the 29th of April, 1847, the last member of that party was brought to Capt. Sutter's Fort: it is utterly impossible to give any description of the sufferings of the company. Your readers can form some idea of them by perusing the above diary.

Yours, &c.

GEORGE McKINSTRY, JR.

Statement of John Sinclair, Esq., Alcalde. District of Sacramento

Rancho del Paso, February, 1847.

Dear Sir,—

The following brief sketch of the sufferings of the emigrants who endeavored at different times to reach this valley from the mountains, where they had been caught by the snow in October, is drawn up at the request of the survivors, with whom I have held several conversations on the subject, and from a few short notes handed me by W. H. Eddy, one of the party. Such as they are, and hastily thrown together, I place them at your disposal.

On the first of November, Patrick Brin, [Breen] Patrick Dolan—Keysburg, [Louis Keseberg] and W. H. Eddy, left their cabins, and attempted to cross the dividing ridge of the mountains; but owing to the softness and depth of the snow, they were obliged to return. On the third they tried it again, taking with them Mrs. Reed and family, Mr. Stanton, and two Indians, who were in the employ of J. A. Sutter; but after being out one day and night, they returned to their cabins. On the twelfth, Mr. Graves, and two daughters, Messrs. Fosdick, Foster, Eddy, Stanton, Sheumacher, [Shoemaker] with two New Mexicans, and the two Indians, started on another trail, but met with no better success. Not discouraged, and impelled by the increasing scarcity of provisions at the cabins, on the twentieth they tried it again, and succeeded in crossing the divide; but found it impossible for them to proceed for the want of a pilot, Mr. Stanton having refused to allow the Indians to accompany them on account of not being able to bring the mules out with them, which Mr. Stanton had taken there with provisions from J. A. Sutter's, previous to the falling of the snow. Here again were their warmest hopes blighted; and they again turned with heavy hearts towards their miserable cabins. Mrs. Murphy, daughter, and two sons were of this party. During the interval between this last attempt and the next, there came on a storm, and the snow fell to the depth of eight feet. In the midst of the storm, two young men started to go to another party of emigrants, (twenty-four in number,) distant about eight miles, who it was known at the commencement of the storm had no cabins built, neither had they killed their cattle, as they still had hopes of being able to cross the mountains. As the two young men never returned, it is supposed they perished in the storm; and it is the opinion of those who have arrived here, that the party to whom they were going must have all perished. On the sixteenth of December, expecting that they would be able to reach the settlements in ten days, Messrs. Graves, Fosdick, Dolan, Foster, Eddy, Stanton, L. Murphy, (aged thirteen,) Antonio, a New Mexican; with Mrs. Fosdick, Mrs. Foster, Mrs. Pike, Mrs. McCutcheon, and Miss M. Graves, and the two Indians before mentioned, having prepared themselves with snow-shoes, again started on their perilous undertaking, determined to succeed or perish.

Those who have ever made an attempt to walk with snow-shoes will be able to realize the difficulty they experienced. On first starting, the snow being so light and loose, even with their snow-shoes, they sank twelve inches at every step; however, they succeeded in travelling about four miles that day. On the seventeenth they crossed the divide, with considerable difficulty and fatigue, making about five miles, the snow on the divide being twelve feet deep. The next day they made six miles, and, on the nineteenth five, it having snowed all day. On the twentieth the sun rose clear and beautiful, and cheered by its sparkling rays, they pursued their weary way. From the first day, Mr. Stanton, it appears, could not keep up with them but had always reached their camp by the time they got their fire built, and preparations made for passing the night. This day they had travelled eight miles, and encamped early; and as the shades of evening gathered round them, many an anxious glance was cast back through the deepening gloom for Stanton; but he came not. Before morning the weather became stormy, and at daylight they started and went about four miles, when they encamped, and agreed to wait and see if Stanton would come up; but that night his place was again vacant by their cheerless fire, while he, I suppose, had escaped from all further suffering, and lay wrapped in his "winding sheet of snow" —

"His weary wand'rings and his travels o'er."

On the twenty-second the storm still continued, and they remained in camp until the twenty-third, when they again started, although the storm still continued, and travelled eight miles. They encamped in a deep valley. Here the appearance of the country was so different from what it had been represented to them, (probably by Mr. Stanton,) that they came to the conclusion that they were lost; and the two Indians on whom they had placed all their confidence, were bewildered. In this melancholy situation they consulted together, and concluded they would go on, trusting in Providence, rather than return to their miserable cabins. They were, also, at this time, out of provisions, and partly agreed, with the exception of Mr. Foster, that in case of necessity, they would cast lots of who should die to preserve the remainder. During the whole of the night it rained and snowed very heavily, and by morning the snow had so increased that they could not travel; while, to add to their sufferings, their fire had been put out by the rain, and all their endeavors to light another proved abortive.

How heart-rending must have been their situation at this time, as they gazed upon each other, shivering and shrinking from the pitiless storm! Oh! how they must have thought of those happy, happy homes, which but a few short months before they had left with buoyant hopes and fond anticipations! Where, oh where were the green and flowery plains which they had heard of, dreampt, and anticipated beholding, in the month of January, in California? Alas! many of that little party were destined never to behold them. Already was death in the midst of them. Antonio died about nine, A. M.; and at eleven o'clock, P. M., Mr. Graves. The feelings of the rest may be imagined, on seeing two of their small party removed by death in a few hours from them, while the thought must have struck home to every bosom, that they too would shortly follow.

In this critical situation, the presence of mind of Mr. Eddy suggested a plan for keeping themselves warm, which is common amongst the trappers of the Rocky Mountains, when in the snow without fire. It is simply to spread a blanket on the snow, when the party, (if small,) with the exception of one, sit down upon it in a circle, closely as possible, their feet piled over one another in the centre, room being left for the person who has to complete the arrangement. As many blankets as necessary are then spread over the heads of the party, the ends being kept down by billets of wood or snow. After every thing is completed, the person outside takes his place in the circle. As the snow falls it closes up the pores of the blankets, while the breath from the party underneath soon causes a comfortable warmth. It was with a great deal of difficulty that Mr. Eddy succeeded in getting them to adopt this simple plan, which undoubtedly was the means of saving their lives at this time. In this situation they remained thirty-six hours.

On the twenty-fifth, about four o'clock, P. M., Patrick Dolan died; he had been for some hours delirious, and escaped from under their shelter, when he stripped off his coat, hat, and boots, and exposed himself to the storm. Mr. Eddy tried to force him back, but his strength was unequal to the task. He, however, afterwards returned of his own accord, and laid down outside of their shelter, when they succeeded in dragging him inside. On the twenty-sixth, L. Murphy died, he likewise being delirious; and was only kept under their shelter by the united strength of the party.

In the afternoon of this day they succeeded in getting fire into a dry pine-tree. Having been four entire days without food, and since the month of October on short allowance, there was now but two alternatives left them—either to die, or preserve life by eating the bodies of the dead: slowly and reluctantly they adopted the latter alternative. On the twenty-seventh they took the flesh from the bodies of the dead; and on that, and the two following days they remained in camp drying the meat, and preparing to pursue their journey. On the thirtieth they left this melancholy spot, where so many of their friends and relatives had perished; and with heavy hearts and dark forebodings of the future pursued their pathless course through the new-fallen snow, and made about five miles: next day about six miles. January first was one of the most fatiguing day's journeys which they had. They were compelled to climb a mountain, which they represent as nearly perpendicular; to accomplish which, they were obliged to take advantage of every cleft of rock, and pull themselves up by shrubs growing in the crevices. On the second they found they could go without snowshoes, which, however, gave them but little relief; their feet being so badly frozen by this time, that every step was marked with blood, and the toes of one of the Indians had dropped off at the first joint. They were also again out of provisions. On the third they travelled seven miles, and at night fared on the strings of their snow-shoes.

Some time during the night of the fourth, the Indians left them; no doubt fearful to remain, lest they might be sacrificed for food. Poor fellows, they stood the pangs of hunger two days longer than their white fellow-travellers before they tasted of the human flesh. On the morning of the fifth, the party took the trail of the Indians, following it by the blood which marked their steps. After having travelled about a mile, they discovered fresh footprints of deer in the snow, when Mr. Eddy, who had a rifle, started with Miss Graves, in advance, hoping to fall in with them, which they fortuntately did, and succeeded in killing one, after travelling about eight miles, at the foot of a mountain. That night Mr. Foster and wife, Mrs. Pike, and Mrs. McCutcheon, encamped on the top of the mountain, not being able to get to where Eddy was with the deer. Mr. Fosdick having given out, remained with his wife about a mile back from them. On the next day they got what remained of the deer to the top of the mountain, and two of them went back for Fosdick; but he was at that time "where the weary are at rest," having died about eleven o'clock, P. M.; and his wife had lain by his side that lonesome night, and prayed that death might release her from suffering, but in vain.

The flesh was taken from the bones of poor Fosdick, and brought into camp, but there was one there who tasted not of it. On the seventh and eighth they only made about two and a half miles, going down one mountain and over another. On the ninth, after travelling four miles, they fell in with the two Indians, who had then got out of the snow, Salvador was dead. Lewis had crawled to a small stream of water, and lain down to drink. They raised him up, and offered him some food; he tried to eat, but could not; and only lived about an hour. Being nearly out of provisions and knowing not how far they might be from the settlements, they took their flesh likewise.

On the tenth and eleventh they made about seventeen miles, when falling in with an Indian trail, they concluded they would follow it, which they accordingly did; and on the twelfth, fell in with some of the Indians, who treated them kindly, gave them some acorns, and put them on to another trail the next day, which they took, and after travelling four miles in a heavy rain-storm, they came to more Indians, with whom they stopped the remainder of that day and the next. The two next days they made about seventeen miles. The seventeenth, after walking two or three miles, with an Indian for a pilot, Mr. Foster and the women gave out, their feet being swollen to such a degree that they could go no further.

Mr. Eddy, who it appears stood the fatigues of the journey better than any of them, here left them; and assisted by two Indians, that evening reached the settlement on bear Creek [Johnson's Rancho.] The inhabitants, on being informed of the situation of the party behind, immediately started with provisions on foot, and reached them that night about twelve o'clock. On the morning of the eighteenth, others started with horses, and brought them to the settlement, where they were treated with every mark of kindness by the inhabitants.

I remain, very respectfully,
Your obd't servant,
JOHN SINCLAIR

**SCHOOL OF EDUCATION
CURRICULUM LABORATORY
UM-DEARBORN**